DELIGHTFUL ANTHOLOGIES

THE OPEN ROAD

Compiled by E. V. LUCAS. A little book for wayfarers containing some 125 poems from over 60 authors.

THE FRIENDLY TOWN

Compiled by E. V. LUCAS. A little book for the urbane containing over 200 selections in verse and prose from 100 authors.

THE POETIC OLD-WORLD

Compiled by MISS L. H. HUMPHREY. Covers Europe, including Spain, Belgium, and the British Isles, in some 200 poems from about 90 poets. Some 30, not originally written in English, are given in both the original and the best available translation.

These three books are uniform, with full gilt flexible covers and pictured cover linings. 16mo. Each, cloth, $1.50 *net*; leather, $2.50 *net*.

POEMS FOR TRAVELERS

Compiled by MARY R. J. DuBOIS. 16mo. Cloth. $1.50 *net*; leather, $2.50 net. Covers France, Germany, Austria, Switzerland, Italy, and Greece in some three hundred poems from about one hundred and thirty poets.

A BOOK OF VERSES FOR CHILDREN

Compiled by E. V. LUCAS. Over 200 poems representing some 80 authors. With decorations by F. D. BEDFORD. *Revised edition.* $2.00. Library edition, $1.00 net.

HENRY HOLT AND COMPANY

PUBLISHERS   NEW YORK

THE OPEN ROAD

A Little Book for Wayfarers

COMPILED BY

E. V. LUCAS

"Life is sweet, brother. . . . There's day and night, brother, both sweet things; sun, moon, and stars, all sweet things; there's likewise a wind on the heath."—*Lavengro.*

NEW YORK
HENRY HOLT AND COMPANY
1909

To B.

Alone, the country life—how sweet!
  But wood and meadow, heath and hill,
The dewy morn, the noonday heat,
The nest half-hid, the poppied wheat,
  The peaty purling rill,
The brake fern's odorous retreat,
The hush of eve, serene, discreet—
  With you are sweeter still.

EXPLANATION

THIS little book aims at nothing but providing companionship on the road for city-dwellers who make holiday. It has no claims to completeness of any kind: it is just a garland of good or enkindling poetry and prose fitted to urge folk into the open air, and, once there, to keep them glad they came—to slip easily from the pocket beneath a tree or among the heather, and provide lazy reading for the time of rest, with perhaps a phrase or two for the feet to step to and the mind to brood on when the rest is over.

E. V. L.

April, 1899.

And hark! how blithe the Throstle sings!
  He, too, is no mean preacher:
Come forth into the light of things,
  Let Nature be your teacher.

She has a world of ready wealth,
  Our minds and hearts to bless—
Spontaneous wisdom breathed by health,
  Truth breathed by cheerfulness.

One impulse from a vernal wood
  May teach you more of man,
Of moral evil and of good,
  Than all the sages can.

Sweet is the lore which Nature brings:
  Our meddling intellect
Misshapes the beauteous form of things;
  We murder to dissect.

Enough of Science and of Art;
  Close up these barren leaves;
Come forth, and bring with you a heart
  That watches and receives.

William Wordsworth.

TABLE OF CONTENTS

FAREWELL TO WINTER AND THE TOWN

		PAGE
THE MEADOWS IN SPRING	Edward Fitzgerald	3
IN CITY STREETS	Ada Smith	6
GOOD COUNSEL	John Davidson	7
THE LAKE ISLE OF INNISFREE	W. B. Yeats	8
THE INVITATION	P. B. Shelley	9

THE ROAD

TITANIA'S COURTESY TO THE WAYFARER	W. Shakespeare	13
ALL DAY A-FOOT	Kenneth Grahame	14
THE VAGABOND	R. L. Stevenson	15
THE WHITE ROAD UP ATHIRT THE HILL	William Barnes	16
THE JOYS OF THE ROAD	Bliss Carman	18
SONG OF THE OPEN ROAD	Walt Whitman	22

SPRING AND THE BEAUTY OF THE EARTH

		PAGE
TURN O' THE YEAR	K. T. Hinkson	43
MARCH	Nora Hopper	44
THE SPRING	William Barnes	44
APRIL	William Watson	46
IN EARLY SPRING	Alice Meynell	46
SONG	Robert Browning	48
LYNTON VERSES	T. E. Brown	48
HOME THOUGHTS FROM ABROAD	Robert Browning	49
A MAY BURDEN	Francis Thompson	50
THE SWEETNESS OF ENGLAND	E. B. Browning	51
(ITALY SWEET TOO!)	John Keats	53
BEAUTY TRIUMPHANT	" "	54
NATURE AND HUMANITY	W. Wordsworth	55
THE RURAL PAN	Kenneth Grahame	57
HYMN OF PAN	P. B. Shelley	58
CALLICLES' SONG	Matthew Arnold	59
BACCHUS	John Keats	62

THE LOVER SINGS

SONG	W. Shakespeare	65
SONG	James Thomson	65
SONG	William Watson	66
THE LADY OF THE LAMBS	Alice Meynell	67
THE MILLER'S DAUGHTER	Alfred Tennyson	68
SONG	Thomas Campion	68
A MATCH	A. C. Swinburne	69

		PAGE
SHE WALKS IN BEAUTY	Lord Byron	71
"MY LUVE IS LIKE A RED, RED ROSE"	Robert Burns	72
SONG	Hartley Coleridge	72
BALLAD	Thomas Hood	73
SONG	James Thomson	74
THE MESSAGE OF THE MARCH WIND	William Morris	75
THE PASSIONATE SHEPHERD TO HIS LOVE	C. Marlowe	76
SONG	Anon.	77
HER BEAUTY	W. Shakespeare	78
CONSTANCY	J. Sylvester	79
SONG	R. Le Gallienne	80

SUN AND CLOUD, AND THE WINDY HILLS

THE SUN	Alice Meynell	83
HYMN OF APOLLO	P. B. Shelley	84
YOUTH AT THE SUMMIT	Maurice Hewlett	86
MORNING ON ETNA	Matthew Arnold	86
THE HORIZON	Alice Meynell	87
THE HILL PANTHEIST	Richard Jefferies	89
"A SMALL SWEET IDYLL"	Alfred Tennyson	91
THE SOUTH-WEST WIND	Alice Meynell	92
ODE TO THE WEST WIND	P. B. Shelley	94
CLOUDS	Alice Meynell	97
THE CLOUD	P. B. Shelley	98
THE DOWNS	Robert Bridges	102

BIRDS, BLOSSOMS, AND TREES

		PAGE
THE VERY BIRDS OF THE AIR	Izaak Walton	107
THE BLACKBIRD	William Barnes	108
SONG	Thomas Heywood	110
THE GREEN LINNET	W. Wordsworth	111
PHILOMELA	Matthew Arnold	113
ODE TO A NIGHTINGALE	John Keats	114
THE DAISIES	Bliss Carman	118
TO THE DAISY	W. Wordsworth	118
TO DAFFODILS	Robert Herrick	120
"I WANDERED LONELY AS A CLOUD"	W. Wordsworth	121
PERDITA'S GIFTS	W. Shakespeare	122
TO PRIMROSES FILLED WITH MORNING DEW	Robert Herrick	124
THE WOODLANDS	William Barnes	126
TAPESTRY TREES	William Morris	127
THE POET IN THE WOODS	William Cowper	128
ON SOLITUDE	Abraham Cowley	129
SONG	W. Shakespeare	132

SUMMER SPORTS AND PASTIMES

A BOY'S PRAYER	H. C. Beeching	134
THE ANGLER'S REST	Izaak Walton	135
THE ANGLER'S VIRTUES	Gervase Markham	141
THE ANGLER'S POESY	Izaak Walton	143
OLD MATCH DAYS	John Nyren	147

		PAGE
THE CRICKET BALL SINGS	E. V. Lucas	150
GOING DOWN HILL ON A BICYCLE	H. C. Beeching	152

REFRESHMENT AND THE INN

THE RESPECT DUE TO HUNGER	W. Hazlitt	157
THE POWER OF MALT	A. E. Housman	158
IN PRAISE OF ALE	Old Song	159
THE MEDITATIVE TANKARD	Edward Fitzgerald	160
TWO RECIPES	Gervase Markham	161
THE HUMBLE FEAST	" "	163
SALVATION YEO'S TESTIMONY TO TOBACCO	Charles Kingsley	164

GARDEN AND ORCHARD

"THE IDLE LIFE I LEAD"	Robert Bridges	168
MY GARDEN	T. E. Brown	169
A GARDEN SONG	Austin Dobson	169
THE GARDEN	Andrew Marvell	170
OF GARDENS	Francis Bacon	173
OF AN ORCHARD	K. T. Hinkson	174
THE APPLE	John Burroughs	175

MUSIC BENEATH A BRANCH

THE SCHOLAR-GIPSY	Matthew Arnold	179
L'ALLEGRO	John Milton	192
SONG	P. B. Shelley	198

		PAGE
"IN THE HIGHLANDS"	R. L. Stevenson	200
THE SOLITARY REAPER	W. Wordsworth	201
RUTH	Thomas Hood	202
CADMUS AND HARMONIA	Matthew Arnold	203
ODE ON A GRECIAN URN	John Keats	205
THE LOTUS-EATERS	Alfred Tennyson	207
THE FORSAKEN MERMAN	Matthew Arnold	210
KUBLA KHAN	S. T. Coleridge	216
LYCIDAS	John Milton	218
ODE ON INTIMATIONS OF IMMORTALITY	W. Wordsworth	226

THE SEA AND THE RIVER

SALT AND SUNNY DAYS	P. B. Marston	239
THE SEA GIPSY	Richard Hovey	240
SAILOR'S SONG	T. L. Beddoes	241
THE WANDER-LOVERS	Richard Hovey	242
THE RIVER AND THE SEA	R. L. Stevenson	244
THE BROOK	Alfred Tennyson	246
AT SEA	R. L. Stevenson	248

THE REDDENING LEAF

TO AUTUMN	John Keats	251
SWEET FERN	J. G. Whittier	253
AUTUMN	R. Le Gallienne	254
CARN A-TURNEN YOLLER	William Barnes	256
"ON WENLOCK EDGE"	A. E. Housman	257
THE JOYS OF FOWLING	Old Song	258
THE MUSIC OF THE PACK	Gervase Markham	259

NIGHT AND THE STARS

		PAGE
"Hail Twilight, Sovereign of One Peaceful Hour"	W. Wordsworth	262
To the Evening Star	William Blake	263
Evemen in the Village	William Barnes	264
Night	William Blake	265
To Night	P. B. Shelley	267
Orion	Kenneth Grahame	268
Sleep Beneath the Stars	R. L. Stevenson	269
To Sleep	W. Wordsworth	271

A LITTLE COMPANY OF GOOD COUNTRY PEOPLE

The Barefoot Boy	J. G. Whittier	275
The Milkmaid	Thomas Nabbes	278
The Shepherd o' the Farm	William Barnes	279
The Shepherd	Maurice Hewlett	281
Walt's Friend	Walt Whitman	281
Tom Sueter	John Nyren	283
Uncle an' Aunt	William Barnes	284
Will Wimble	Addison's 'Spectator'	286
A Gentleman of the Old School	Austin Dobson	288
Mr. Hastings	William Gilpin	292
Jack	E. V. Lucas	295
The Vicar	W. M. Praed	300
The Fiddler of Dooney	W. B. Yeats	304

A HANDFUL OF PHILOSOPHY

		PAGE
THE WORLD IS TOO MUCH WITH US	W. Wordsworth	308
CONTENT	Thomas Dekker	309
THE WISH	Abraham Cowley	310
GIVE ME THE OLD	R. H. Messinger	311
TO-MORROW	John Collins	314
A THANKSGIVING TO GOD	Robert Herrick	315
THE DIRGE IN "CYMBELINE"	W. Shakespeare	318

THE RETURN

THE GLAMOUR OF THE TOWN	Charles Lamb	320
NOTE OF ACKNOWLEDGMENT		323
UP-HILL	Christina Rossetti	326

The decorative end-papers are from original designs by William Hyde.

THE FAREWELL TO WINTER
AND THE TOWN

Come, spur away,
   I have no patience for a longer stay,
   But must go down,
And leave the chargeable noise of this great town
   I will the country see . . .
                              Thomas Randolph.

Oh, day, if I squander a wavelet of thee,
A mite of my twelve hours' treasure,
The least of thy gazes or glances . . .
The shame fall on Asolo, mischief on me!
Thy long, blue, solemn hours serenely flowing,
Whence earth, we feel, gets steady help and good—
Thy fitful sunshine minutes, coming, going,
As if earth turned from work in gamesome mood,
All shall be mine! . . .
            Robert Browning (Pippa Passes).

O the gleesome saunter over fields and hillsides!
The leaves and flowers of the commonest weeds, the moist fresh stillness of the woods,
The exquisite smell of the earth at daybreak, and all through the forenoon.
                              Walt Whitman.

THE OPEN ROAD

The Meadows in Spring ～ ～ ～

'TIS a dull sight
    To see the year dying,
When winter winds
    Set the yellow wood sighing:
        Sighing, oh! sighing.

When such a time cometh,
    I do retire
Into an old room
    Beside a bright fire:
        Oh, pile a bright fire!

And there I sit
    Reading old things,
Of knights and lorn damsels,
    While the wind sings—
        Oh, drearily sings!

I never look out
    Nor attend to the blast;

For all to be seen
  Is the leaves falling fast:
    Falling, falling!

But close at the hearth,
  Like a cricket, sit I,
Reading of summer
  And chivalry—
    Gallant chivalry!

Then with an old friend
  I talk of our youth—
How 'twas gladsome, but often
  Foolish, forsooth:
    But gladsome, gladsome!

Or to get merry
  We sing some old rhyme,
That made the wood ring again
  In summer time—
    Sweet summer time!

Then go we to smoking,
  Silent and snug:
Nought passes between us,
  Save a brown jug—
    Sometimes!

And sometimes a tear
  Will rise in each eye,

Seeing the two old friends
　So merrily—
　　　So merrily!

And ere to bed
　Go we, go we,
Down on the ashes
　We kneel on the knee,
　　　Praying together!

Thus, then, live I,
　Till, 'mid all the gloom,
By heaven! the bold sun
　Is with me in the room
　　　Shining, shining!

Then the clouds part,
　Swallows soaring between;
The spring is alive,
　And the meadows are green!

I jump up, like mad,
　Break the old pipe in twain,
And away to the meadows,
　The meadows again!
　　　　　　　Edward FitzGerald.

In City Streets

YONDER in the heather there's a bed for sleeping,
  Drink for one athirst, ripe blackberries to eat;
Yonder in the sun the merry hares go leaping,
  And the pool is clear for travel-wearied feet.

Sorely throb my feet, a-tramping London highways,
  (Ah! the springy moss upon a northern moor!)
Through the endless streets, the gloomy squares and byways,
  Homeless in the City, poor among the poor!

London streets are gold—ah, give me leaves a-glinting
  'Midst grey dykes and hedges in the autumn sun!
London water's wine, poured out for all unstinting—
  God! For the little brooks that tumble as they run!

Oh, my heart is fain to hear the soft wind blowing,
  Soughing through the fir-tops up on northern fells!

Oh, my eye's an ache to see the brown burns
   flowing
   Through the peaty soil and tinkling heather-
      bells.
Ada Smith.

Good Counsel

(From *Fleet Street Eclogues*)

At early dawn through London you must go
   Until you come where long black
      hedgerows grow,
With pink buds pearled, and here and there a
   tree,
And gates and stiles; and watch good country
   folk;
And scent the spicy smoke
Of withered weeds that burn where gardens be;
And in a ditch perhaps a primrose see.

The rooks shall stalk the plough, larks mount
   the skies,
Blackbirds and speckled thrushes sing aloud,
Hid in the warm white cloud
Mantling the thorn, and far away shall rise
The milky low of cows, and farm-yard cries.
John Davidson.

The Lake Isle of Innisfree

I WILL arise and go now, and go to Innisfree,
 And a small cabin build there, of clay and wattles made;
Nine bean rows will I have there, a hive for the honey bee,
 And live alone in the bee-loud glade.

And I shall have some peace there, for peace comes dropping slow,
 Dropping from the veils of the morning to where the cricket sings;
There midnight's all a glimmer, and noon a purple glow,
 And evening full of the linnet's wings.

I will arise and go now, for always, night and day,
 I hear lake-water lapping with low sounds by the shore;
While I stand on the roadway or on the pavements gray,
 I hear it in the deep heart's core.

W. B. Yeats

The Invitation

BEST and brightest, come away,—
    Fairer far than this fair Day,
Which, like thee, to those in sorrow
Comes to bid a sweet good-morrow
To the rough year just awake
In its cradle on the brake.
The brightest hour of unborn Spring
Through the winter wandering,
Found, it seems, the halcyon morn
To hoar February born;
Bending from Heaven, in azure mirth,
It kiss'd the forehead of the earth,
And smiled upon the silent sea,
And bade the frozen streams be free,
And waked to music all their fountains,
And breathed upon the frozen mountains,
And like the prophetess of May
Strew'd flowers upon the barren way,
Making the wintry world appear
Like one on whom thou smilest, dear.

Away, away, from men and towns,
To the wild wood and the downs—
To the silent wilderness
Where the soul need not repress
Its music, lest it should not find
An echo in another's mind,

While the touch of Nature's art
Harmonizes heart to heart.

    Radiant Sister of the Day
Awake! arise! and come away!
To the wild woods and the plains,
To the pools where winter rains
Image all their roof of leaves,
Where the pine its garland weaves
Of sapless green, and ivy dun,
Round stems that never kiss the sun;
Where the lawns and pastures be
And the sandhills of the sea;
Where the melting hoar-frost wets
The daisy-star that never sets,
And wind-flowers and violets
Which yet join not scent to hue
Crown the pale year weak and new;
When the night is left behind
In the deep east, dim and blind,
And the blue moon is over us,
And the multitudinous
Billows murmur at our feet,
Where the earth and ocean meet,
And all things seem only one
In the universal Sun.
Percy Bysshe Shelley.

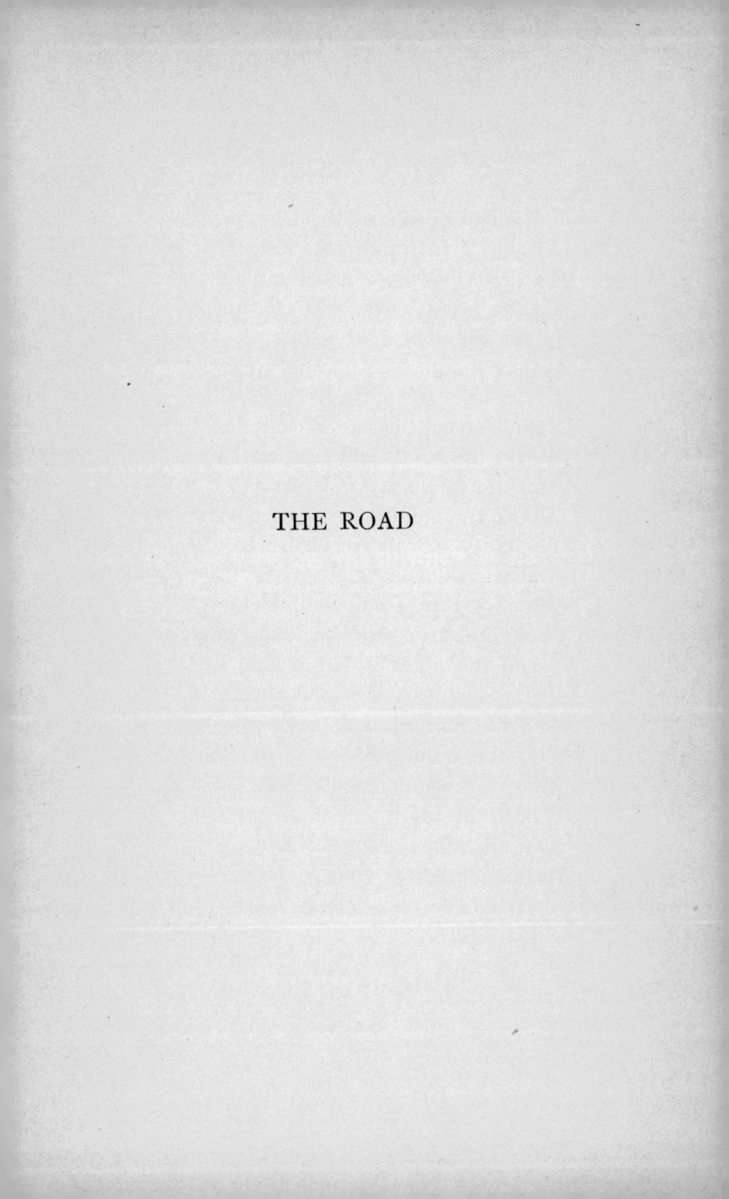

THE ROAD

In its widest sense, "the open road" is the sign and symbol of all outdoor life, of all holiday-making in which the sense of the athlete is awakened,—in a word, of all that is active and adventurous, from sailing and rowing to cliff-climbing and moorland tramping. But fascinating as these are, there is a something even more fascinating in the thought of the open road when we narrow the meaning and confine it to the paths trod by the feet of men and horses and cut by their wheels, restrict it, that is, to those nerves and sinews of the soil which bind village to village, city to city, and land to land. Think of all the many and diverse tracks which, once landed at Calais, if only you keep going eastward, will take you to Moscow or Tobolsk, westward to Lisbon or Madrid, and southward to Rome. What is more intellectually exhilarating to the mind, and even to the senses, than to stand looking down the vista of some great road in France or Italy, or up a long and well-worn horse-track in Asia or Africa, a path which has not yet been trod by the foot or the wheel of the gazing wayfarer, or by the hoof of his horse, and to wonder through what strange places, by what towns and castles, by what rivers and streams, by what mountains and valleys it will take him ere he reaches his destination?

The Spectator.

Titania's Courtesy to the Wayfarer

(From *A Midsummer-Night's Dream*)

TITANIA. Peas-blossom! Cobweb! Moth!
and Mustard-seed!
  (*Enter four Fairies.*)
First Fairy. Ready.
Second Fairy. And I.
Third Fairy. And I.
Fourth Fairy. Where shall we go?
Titania. Be kind and courteous to this gentleman;
Hop in his walks, and gambol in his eyes;
Feed him with apricocks, and dewberries;
With purple grapes, green figs, and mulberries;
The honey bags steal from the humble bees,
And, for night-tapers, crop their waxen thighs,
And light them at the fiery glow-worm's eyes,
To have my love to bed, and to arise;

And pluck the wings from painted butterflies,
To fan the moonbeams from his sleeping eyes;
Nod to him, elves, and do him courtesies.
                    William Shakespeare.

All Day A-foot

(From *Pagan Papers*)

A DAY'S *Ride a Life's Romance* was the excellent title of an unsuccessful book; and indeed the journey should march with the day, beginning and ending with its sun, to be the complete thing, the golden round required of it. This makes that mind and body fare together, hand in hand, sharing the hope, the action, the fruition; finding equal sweetness in the languor of aching limbs at eve, and in the first god-like intoxication of motion with braced muscle in the sun. For walk or ride take the mind over greater distances than a throbbing whirl with stiffening joints and cramped limbs through a dozen counties. Surely you seem to cover vaster spaces with Lavengro, footing it with gypsies or driving his tinker's cart across lonely commons, than with many a globe-trotter or steam-yachtsman with diary or log?
                    Kenneth Grahame.

The Vagabond

(To an air of Schubert)

Give to me the life I love,
  Let the lave go by me,
Give the jolly heaven above
  And the byway nigh me.
Bed in the bush with stars to see,
  Bread I dip in the river—
There's the life for a man like me,
  There's the life for ever.

Let the blow fall soon or late,
  Let what will be o'er me;
Give the face of earth around
  And the road before me.
Wealth I seek not, hope nor love,
  Nor a friend to know me;
All I seek, the heaven above
  And the road below me.

Or let autumn fall on me
  Where afield I linger,
Silencing the bird on tree,
  Biting the blue finger.
White as meal the frosty field—
  Warm the fireside haven—
Not to autumn will I yield,
  Not to winter even!

Let the blow fall soon or late,
  Let what will be o'er me;
Give the face of earth around,
  And the road before me.
Wealth I ask not, hope nor love,
  Nor a friend to know me;
All I ask, the heaven above
  And the road below me.
                Robert Louis Stevenson.

The White Road up Athirt the Hill ◠ ◠

WHEN high hot zuns 'da strik right down,
An' burn our zweaty fiazen brown,
An' zunny hangèns that be nigh
Be back'd by hills so blue's the sky;
Then while the bells da sweetly cheem
Upon the champèn high-neck'd team
How lively, wi' a friend, da seem
  The white road up athirt the hill.

The zwellèn downs, wi' chaky tracks,
A-climmèn up ther zunny backs,
Da hide green meäds, an' zedgy brooks,
An' clumps o' trees wi' glossy rooks,

An' hearty vo'ke to lafe and zing,
An' churches wi' ther bells to ring,
In parishes al in a string
    Wi' white roads up athirt the hills.

At feäst, when uncle's vo'ke da come
To spend the da wi' we at huome,
An' we da put upon the buard
The best of al we can avvuord,
The wolden oons do ta'ke an' smoke,
An' younger oons da play an' joke,
An' in the evemen all our vo'ke
    Da bring 'em gwáin athirt the hill.

Var then the green da zwarm wi' wold
An' young so thick as sheep in vuold.
The billis in the blacksmith's shop
An' mesh-green waterwheel da stop,
An' luonesome in the wheelwright's shed
's a-left the wheelless waggon bed,
While zwarms o' comen-friends da tread
    The white road down athirt the hill.

An' when the winden road so white
A-climmen up the hill in zight,
Da leäd to pliazen, east ar west
The vust a-know'd an' lov'd the best,

How touchèn in the zunsheen's glow
Ar in the shiades that clouds da drow
Upon the zunburn'd down below,
    's the white road up athirt the hill.

What pirty hollers now the long
White roads da windy roun' among,
Wi' dairy cows in woody nooks,
An' hâymiakers among ther pooks,
An' housen that the trees da screen
Vrom zun an' zight by boughs o' green,
Young blushèn beauty's huomes between
    The white roads up athirt the hills.
William Barnes.

The Joys of the Road

NOW the joys of the road are chiefly these:
A crimson touch on the hard-wood trees;

A vagrant's morning wide and blue,
In early fall, when the wind walks, too;

A shadowy highway cool and brown,
Alluring up and enticing down

From rippled water to dappled swamp,
From purple glory to scarlet pomp;

The outward eye, the quiet will,
And the striding heart from hill to hill;

The tempter apple over the fence;
The cobweb bloom on the yellow quince;

The palish asters along the wood,—
A lyric touch of the solitude;

An open hand, an easy shoe,
And a hope to make the day go through,—

Another to sleep with, and a third
To wake me up at the voice of a bird,

The resonant far-listening morn,
And the hoarse whisper of the corn;

The crickets mourning their comrades lost,
In the night's retreat from the gathering frost;

(Or is it their slogan, plaintive and shrill,
As they beat on their corselets, valiant still?)

A hunger fit for the kings of the sea,
And a loaf of bread for Dickon and me;

A thirst like that of the Thirsty Sword,
And a jug of cider on the board;

An idle noon, a bubbling spring,
The sea in the pine-tops murmuring;

A scrap of gossip at the ferry;
A comrade neither glum nor merry,

Asking nothing, revealing naught,
But minting his words from a fund of thought,

A keeper of silence eloquent,
Needy, yet royally well content,

Of the mettled breed, yet abhorring strife,
And full of the mellow juice of life,

A taster of wine, with an eye for a maid,
Never too bold, and never afraid,

Never heart-whole, never heart-sick
(These are the things I worship in Dick)

No fidget and no reformer, just
A calm observer of ought and must,

A lover of books, but a reader of man,
No cynic and no charlatan,

Who never defers and never demands,
But, smiling, takes the world in his hands,—

Seeing it good as when God first saw
And gave it the weight of His will for law.

And O the joy that is never won,
But follows and follows the journeying sun,

By marsh and tide, by meadow and stream,
A will-o'-the-wind, a light-o'-dream,

Delusion afar, delight anear,
From morrow to morrow, from year to year.

A jack-o'-lantern, a fairy fire,
A dare, a bliss, and a desire!

The racy smell of the forest loam,
When the stealthy, sad-heart leaves go home;

(O leaves, O leaves, I am one with you,
Of the mould and the sun and the wind and
 the dew!)

The broad gold wake of the afternoon;
The silent fleck of the cold new moon;

The sound of the hollow sea's release
From stormy tumult to starry peace;

With only another league to wend;
And two brown arms at the journey's end!

These are the joys of the open road—
For him who travels without a load.
      Bliss Carman.

Song of the Open Road

I

AFOOT and light-hearted I take to the open road,
Healthy, free, the world before me,
The long brown path before me leading wherever I choose.

Henceforth I ask not good-fortune, I myself am good-fortune,
Henceforth I whimper no more, postpone no more, need nothing,
Done with indoor complaints, libraries, querulous criticisms,
Strong and content I travel the open road.

The earth, that is sufficient,
I do not want the constellations any nearer,
I know they are very well where they are,
I know they suffice for those who belong to them.

(Still here I carry my old delicious burdens,
I carry them, men and women, I carry them with me wherever I go,
I swear it is impossible for me to get rid of them,
I am fill'd with them, and I will fill them in return.)

2

You road I enter upon and look around, I believe you are not all that is here,
I believe that much unseen is also here.

Here the profound lesson of reception, nor preference nor denial,
The black with his woolly head, the felon, the diseas'd, the illiterate person, are not denied;
The birth, the hasting after the physician, the beggar's tramp, the drunkard's stagger, the laughing party of mechanics,
The escaped youth, the rich person's carriage, the fop, the eloping couple,
The early market-man, the hearse, the moving of furniture into the town, the return back from the town,
They pass, I also pass, any thing passes, none can be interdicted,
None but are accepted, none but shall be dear to me.

3

You air that serves me with breath to speak!
You objects that call from diffusion my meanings and give them shape!

You light that wraps me and all things in delicate equable showers!
You paths worn in the irregular hollows by the roadsides!
I believe you are latent with unseen existences, you are so dear to me.

You flagg'd walks of the cities! you strong curbs at the edges!
You ferries! you planks and posts of wharves! you timber-lined sides! you distant ships!
You rows of houses! you window-pierced facades! you roofs!
You porches and entrances! you copings and iron guards!
You windows whose transparent shells might expose so much!
You doors and ascending steps! you arches!
You grey stones of interminable pavements! you trodden crossings!
From all that has touch'd you I believe you have imparted to yourselves, and now would impart the same secretly to me,
From the living and the dead you have peopled your impassive surfaces, and the spirits thereof would be evident and amicable with me.

4

The earth expanding right hand and left hand,
The picture alive, every part in its best light,
The music falling in where it is wanted, and stopping where it is not wanted,
The cheerful voice of the public road, the gay fresh sentiment of the road.

O highway I travel, do you say to me *Do not leave me?*
Do you say *Venture not—if you leave me you are lost?*
Do you say *I am already prepared, I am well beaten and undenied, adhere to me?*

O public road, I say back I am not afraid to leave you, yet I love you,
You express me better than I can express myself,
You shall be more to me than my poem.

I think heroic deeds were all conceiv'd in the open air, and all free poems also,
I think I could stop here myself and do miracles,
I think whatever I shall meet on the road I shall like, and whoever beholds me shall like me,
I think whoever I see must be happy.

5

From this hour I ordain myself loos'd of limits
and imaginary lines,
Going where I list, my own master total and
absolute,

Listening to others, considering well what they
say,
Pausing, searching, receiving, contemplating,
Gently, but with undeniable will, divesting myself of the holds that would hold me.

I inhale great draughts of space,
The east and the west are mine, and the north
and the south are mine.

I am larger, better than I thought,
I did not know I held so much goodness.

All seems beautiful to me,
I can repeat over to men and women You have
done such good to me I would do the
same to you,
I will recruit for myself and you as I go,
I will scatter myself among men and women
as I go,

I will toss a new gladness and roughness among them,
Whoever denies me it shall not trouble me,
Whoever accepts me he or she shall be blessed and shall bless me.

6

Now if a thousand perfect men were to appear it would not amaze me,
Now if a thousand beautiful forms of women appear'd it would not astonish me.

Now I see the secret of the making of the best persons,
It is to grow in the open air and to eat and sleep with the earth.

Here a great personal deed has room,
(Such a deed seizes upon the hearts of the whole race of men,
Its effusion of strength and will overwhelms laws and mocks all authority and all argument against it).

Here is the test of wisdom:
Wisdom is not finally tested in schools,
Wisdom cannot be pass'd from one having it to another not having it,

Wisdom is of the soul, is not susceptible of
    proof, is its own proof,
Applies to all stages and objects and qualities
    and is content,
Is the certainty of the reality and immortality
    of things, and the excellence of things;
Something there is in the float of the sight of
    things that provokes it out of the soul.

Now I re-examine philosophies and religions,
They may prove well in lecture-rooms, yet not
    prove at all under the spacious clouds
    and along the landscape and flowing
    currents.

Here is realisation,
Here is a man tallied—he realises here what
    he has in him,
The past, the future, majesty, love—if they
    are vacant of you, you are vacant of
    them.

Only the kernel of every object nourishes;
Where is he who tears off the husks for you
    and me?
Where is he that undoes stratagems and en-
    velopes for you and me?

Here is adhesiveness, it is not previously
    fashion'd, it is apropos;
Do you know what it is as you pass to be loved
    by strangers?
Do you know the talk of those turning eye-
    balls?

7

Here is the efflux of the soul,
The efflux of the soul comes from within
    through embower'd gates, ever provok-
    ing questions,
These yearnings, why are they? these thoughts
    in the darkness, why are they?
Why are there men and women that while
    they are nigh me the sunlight expands
    my blood?
Why when they leave me do my pennants of
    joy sink flat and lank?

Why are there trees I never walk under but
    large and melodious thoughts descend
    upon me?
(I think they hang there winter and summer
    on those trees and always drop fruit as
    I pass;)
What is it I interchange so suddenly with
    strangers?

What with some driver as I ride on the seat
  by his side?
What with some fisherman drawing his seine
  by the shore as I walk by and pause?
What gives me to be free to a woman's and
  man's good-will? what gives them to be
  free to mine?

8

The efflux of the soul is happiness, here is
  happiness,
I think it pervades the open air, waiting at all
  times,
Now it flows unto us, we are rightly charged.

Here rises the fluid and attaching character,
The fluid and attaching character is the freshness and sweetness of man and woman,
(The herbs of the morning sprout no fresher
  and sweeter every day out of the roots
  of themselves, than it sprouts fresh and
  sweet continually out of itself).

Toward the fluid and attaching character
  exudes the sweat of the love of young
  and old,

From it falls distill'd the charm that mocks beauty and attainments,
Toward it heaves the shuddering longing ache of contact.

9

Allons! Whoever you are, come travel with me!
Travelling with me you find what never tires.

The earth never tires,
The earth is rude, silent, incomprehensible at first,
Nature is rude and incomprehensible at first,
Be not discouraged, keep on, there are divine things well envelop'd,
I swear to you there are divine things more beautiful than words can tell.

Allons! we must not stop here,
However sweet these laid-up stores, however convenient this dwelling, we cannot remain here,
However shelter'd this port and however calm these waters, we must not anchor here,
However welcome the hospitality that surrounds us, we are permitted to receive it but a little while.

Allons! the inducements shall be greater,
We will sail pathless and wild seas,
We will go where winds blow, waves dash, and the Yankee clipper speeds by under full sail.

Allons! with power, liberty, the earth, the elements,
Health, defiance, gaiety, self-esteem, curiosity;
Allons! from all formules!
From your formules, O bat-eyed and materialistic priests.

The stale cadaver blocks up the passage—the burial waits no longer.

Allons! yet take warning!
He travelling with me needs the best blood, thews, endurance,
None may come to the trial till he or she bring courage and health,
Come not here if you have already spent the best of yourself,
Only those may come who come in sweet and determin'd bodies,

No diseas'd person, no rum drinker or venereal
    taint is permitted here.
(I and mine do not convince by arguments,
    similes, rhymes,
We convince by our presence.)

II

Listen! I will be honest with you:
I do not offer the old smooth prizes, but offer
    rough new prizes,
These are the days that must happen to you:
You shall not heap up what is call'd riches,
You shall scatter with lavish hand all that you
    earn or achieve,
You but arrive at the city to which you were
    destin'd, you hardly settle yourself to
    satisfaction before you are call'd by an
    irresistible call to depart,
You shall be treated to the ironical smiles and
    mockings of those who remain behind
    you,
What beckonings of love you receive you shall
    only answer with passionate kisses of
    parting,
You shall not allow the hold of those who
    spread their reach'd hands toward you.

12

Allons! after the great Companions, and to belong to them!
They too are on the road—they are the swift and majestic men—they are the greatest women,
Enjoyers of calms of seas and storms of seas,
Sailors of many a ship, walkers of many a mile of land,
Habitués of many distant countries, habitués of far distant dwelling,
Trusters of men and women, observers of cities, solitary toilers,
Pausers and contemplators of tufts, blossoms, shells of the shore,
Dancers at wedding-dances, kissers of brides, tender helpers of children, bearers of children,
Soldiers of revolts, standers by gaping graves, lowerers-down of coffins,
Journeyers over consecutive seasons, over the years, the curious years each emerging from that which preceded it,
Journeyers as with companions, namely their own diverse phases,
Forth-steppers from the latent unrealised baby-days,

Journeyers gaily with their own youth, journeyers with their bearded and well-grain'd manhood,
Journeyers with their womanhood, ample, unsurpass'd, content,
Journeyers with their own sublime old age, of manhood and womanhood,
Old age, calm, expanded, broad with the haughty breadth of the universe,
Old age, flowing free with the delicious nearby freedom of death.

13

Allons! to that which is endless as it was beginningless,
To undergo much, tramps of days, rests of nights,
To merge all in the travel they tend to, and the days and nights they tend to,
Again to merge them in the start of superior journeys,
To see nothing anywhere but what you may reach it and pass it,
To conceive no time, however distant, but what you may reach it and pass it,
To look up or down no road but it stretches and waits for you, however long but it stretches and waits for you,

To see no being, not God's or any, but you also
  go thither,
To see no possession but you may possess it,
  enjoying all without labour or purchase,
  abstracting the feast yet not abstracting
  one particle of it,
To take the best of the farmer's farm and the
  rich man's elegant villa, and the chaste
  blessings of the well-married couple,
  and the fruits of orchards and flowers
  of gardens,
To take to your use out of the compact cities
  as you pass through,
To carry buildings and streets with you after-
  ward wherever you go,
To gather the minds of men out of their
  brains as you encounter them, to gather
  the love out of their hearts,
To take your lovers on the road with you, for
  all that you leave them behind you,
To know the universe itself as a road, as many
  roads, as roads for travelling souls.

All parts away for the progress of souls,
All religion, all solid things, arts, governments
  —all that was or is apparent upon this
  globe or any globe, falls into niches and
  corners before the procession of souls
  along the grand roads of the universe.

Of the progress of the souls of men and women
along the grand roads of the universe,
all other progress is the needed emblem
and sustenance.

Forever alive, forever forward,
Stately, solemn, sad, withdrawn, baffled, mad,
turbulent, feeble, dissatisfied,
Desperate, proud, fond, sick, accepted by men,
rejected by men,
They go! they go! I know that they go, but
I know not where they go,
But I know that they go toward the best—
toward something great.

Whoever you are, come forth! or man or
woman, come forth!
You must not stay sleeping and dallying there
in the house, though you built it, or
though it has been built for you.

Out of the dark confinement! out from behind
the screen!
It is useless to protest, I know all and expose it.

Behold through you as bad as the rest,
Through the laughter, dancing, dining, supping, of people,

Inside of dresses and ornaments, inside of those wash'd and trimm'd faces,
Behold a secret silent loathing and despair.

No husband, no wife, no friend, trusted to hear the confession,
Another self, a duplicate of every one, skulking and hiding it goes,
Formless and wordless through the streets of the cities, polite and bland in the parlours,
In the cars of railroads, in steamboats, in the public assembly,
Home to the houses of men and women, at the table, in the bed-room, everywhere,
Smartly attired, countenance smiling, form upright, death under the breast-bones, hell under the skull-bones,
Under the broadcloth and gloves, under the ribbons and artificial flowers,
Keeping fair with the customs, speaking not a syllable of itself.
Speaking of any thing else, but never of itself.

14

Allons! through struggles and wars!
The goal that was named cannot be countermanded.

Have the past struggles succeeded?
What has succeeded? yourself? your nation? Nature?
Now understand me well—it is provided in the essence of things that from any fruition of success, no matter what, shall come forth something to make a greater struggle necessary.

My call is the call of battle, I nourish active rebellion,
He going with me must go well arm'd,
He going with me goes often with spare diet, poverty, angry enemies, desertions.

15

Allons! the road is before us!
It is safe—I have tried it—my own feet have tried it well—be not detain'd!

Let the paper remain on the desk unwritten, and the book on the shelf unopen'd!
Let the tools remain in the workshop! let the money remain unearn'd!
Let the school stand! mind not the cry of the teacher!
Let the preacher preach in his pulpit! let the lawyer plead in the court, and the judge expound the law.

Camerado, I will give you my hand!
I give you my love more precious than money,
I give you myself before preaching or law;
Will you give me yourself? will you come travel with me?
Shall we stick by each other as long as we live?

Walt Whitman.

SPRING AND THE BEAUTY
OF THE EARTH

One passage in your Letter a little displeas'd me. The rest was nothing but kindness, which Robert's letters are ever brimful of. You say that "this World to you seems drain'd of all its sweets!" At first I had hoped you only meant to intimate the high price of Sugar! but I am afraid you meant more. O, Robert, I don't know what you call sweet. Honey and the honeycomb, roses and violets, are yet in the earth. The sun and moon yet reign in Heaven, and the lesser lights keep up their pretty twinklings. Meats and drinks, sweet sights and sweet smells, a country walk, spring and autumn, follies and repentance, quarrels and reconcilements have all a sweetness by turns. Good humour and good nature, friends at home that love you, and friends abroad that miss you—you possess all these things, and more innumerable, and these are all sweet things. You may extract honey from everything.

Charles Lamb to Robert Lloyd.

Turn o' the Year ◡ ◡ ◡

THIS is the time when bit by bit
  The days begin to lengthen sweet,
And every minute gained is joy—
And love stirs in the heart of a boy.

This is the time the sun, of late
Content to lie abed till eight,
Lifts up betimes his sleepy head—
And love stirs in the heart of a maid.

This is the time we dock the night
Of a whole hour of candlelight;
When song of linnet and thrush is heard—
And love stirs in the heart of a bird.

This is the time when sword-blades green,
With gold and purple damascene,
Pierce the brown crocus-bed a-row—
And love stirs in a heart I know.
         Katharine Tynan Hinkson.

March

B LOSSOM on the plum,
  Wild wind and merry;
Leaves upon the cherry,
And one swallow come.

Red windy dawn,
  Swift rain and sunny;
Wild bees seeking honey,
Crocus on the lawn;
  Blossom on the plum.

Grass begins to grow,
  Dandelions come;
Snowdrops haste to go
After last month's snow;
Rough winds beat and blow,
  Blossom on the plum.

Nora Hopper.

The Spring

WHEN wintry weather's al a-done
  An' brooks da sparkle in the zun,
An' nâisy buildèn rooks da vlee
Wi' sticks toward ther elem tree,
An' we can hear birds zing, and zee
  Upon the boughs the buds o' spring,
  Then I don't envy any king,
    A-vield wi' health an' zunsheen.

Var then the cowslip's hangèn flow'r,
A-wetted in the zunny show'r,
Da grow wi' vilets sweet o' smell,
That mâidens al da like so well;
An' drushes' aggs, wi' sky-blue shell,
    Da lie in mossy nests among
      The tharns, while the da zing ther zong
        At evemen in the zunsheen.

An' God da miake His win' to blow
An' râin to val var high an' low,
An' tell His marnen zun to rise
Var al alik'; an' groun' an' skies
Ha' colors var the poor man's eyes;
    An' in our trials He is near
    To hear our muoan an' zee our tear,
      An' turn our clouds to zunsheen.

An' many times, when I da vind
Things goo awry, and vo'ke unkind;
To zee the quiet veedèn herds,
An' hear the zingèn o' the birds,
Da still my spurrit muore than words,
    Var I da zee that 'tis our sin
    Da miake oon's soul so dark 'ithin
      When God wood gie us zunsheen.
              William Barnes.

April

APRIL, April,
  Laugh thy girlish laughter;
Then, the moment after,
Weep thy girlish tears!
April, that mine ears
Like a lover greetest,
If I tell thee, sweetest,
All my hopes and fears,
April, April,
Laugh thy golden laughter,
But, the moment after,
Weep thy golden tears!

William Watson.

In Early Spring

O SPRING, I know thee! Seek for sweet surprise
  In the young children's eyes.
But I have learnt the years, and know the yet
  Leaf-folded violet.
Mine ear, awake to silence, can foretell
  The cuckoo's fitful bell.
I wander in a grey time that encloses
  June and the wild hedge-roses.
A year's procession of the flowers doth pass
  My feet, along the grass.
And all you sweet birds silent yet, I know
  The notes that stir you so,

Your songs yet half devised in the dim dear
    Beginnings of the year.
In these young days you meditate your part;
    I have it all by heart.
I know the secrets of the seeds of flowers
    Hidden and warm with showers,
And how, in kindling Spring, the cuckoo shall
    Alter his interval.
But not a flower or song I ponder is
    My own, but memory's.
I shall be silent in those days desired
    Before a world inspired.
O dear brown birds, compose your old song-phrases,
    Earth, thy familiar daisies.

The poet mused upon the dusky height,
    Between two stars towards night,
His purpose in his heart. I watched, a space,
    The meaning of his face:
There was the secret, fled from earth and skies,
    Hid in his grey young eyes.
My heart and all the Summer wait his choice,
    And wonder for his voice.
Who shall foretell his songs, and who aspire
    But to divine his lyre?
Sweet earth, we know thy dimmest mysteries,
    But he is lord of his.

                Alice Meynell.

Song

(From *Pippa Passes*)

THE year's at the spring
    And day's at the morn;
Morning's at seven;
The hill-side's dew-pearled;
The lark's on the wing;
The snail's on the thorn:
God's in His heaven—
All's right with the world!
              Robert Browning.

Lynton Verses

SWEET breeze that sett'st the summer buds a-swaying,
Dear lambs amid the primrose meadows playing,
    Let me not think!
    O floods upon whose brink
  The merry birds are maying,
Dream, softly dream! O blessed mother, lead me
Unsevered from thy girdle—lead me! feed me!
    I have no will but thine;
      I need not but the juice
    Of elemental wine—
      Perish remoter use

Of strength reserved for conflict yet to come!
Let me be dumb,
> As long as I may feel thy hand—
> This, this is all—do ye not understand
How the great Mother mixes all our bloods?
> O breeze! O swaying buds!
> O lambs, O primroses, O floods!
>> *Thomas Edward Brown.*

Home Thoughts from Abroad

OH, to be in England now that April's there,
And whoever wakes in England sees,
   some morning unaware,
That the lowest boughs and the brushwood sheaf
Round the elm-tree bole are in tiny leaf,
While the chaffinch sings on the orchard bough
In England—now!
And after April, when May follows
And the white-throat builds, and all the swallows!
Hark, where my blossomed pear-tree in the hedge
Leans to the field and scatters on the clover
Blossoms and dewdrops—at the bent spray's edge—
That's the wise thrush: he sings each song twice over

Lest you should think he never could recapture
The first fine careless rapture!
And, though the fields look rough with hoary
    dew,
All will be gay when noontide wakes anew
The buttercups, the little children's dower
—Far brighter than this gaudy melon-flower!
                                    Robert Browning.

A May Burden

THROUGH meadow-ways as I did
        tread,
The corn grew in great lustihead,
And hey! the beeches burgeonéd.
    By Goddés fay, by Goddés fay!
It is the month, the jolly month,
It is the jolly month of May.

God ripe the wines and corn, I say,
And wenches for the marriage-day,
And boys to teach love's comely play.
    By Goddés fay, by Goddés fay!
It is the month, the jolly month,
It is the jolly month of May.

As I went down by lane and lea,
The daisies reddened so, pardie!

"Blushets!" I said, "I well do see,
    By Goddés fay, by Goddés fay!
The thing ye think of in this month,
Heigho! this jolly month of May."

As down I went by rye and oats,
The blossoms smelt of kisses; throats
Of birds turned kisses into notes;
    By Goddés fay, by Goddés fay!
The kiss it is a growing flower,
I trow, this jolly month of May.

God send a mouth to every kiss,
Seeing the blossom of this bliss
By gathering doth grow, certes!
    By Goddés fay, by Goddés fay!
Thy brow-garland pushed all aslant
Tells—but I tell not, wanton May!
            Francis Thompson.

The Sweetness of England

(From *Aurora Leigh*)

                A<small>ND</small> when at last
Escaped, so many a green slope built on slope
Betwixt me and the enemy's house behind,
I dared to rest, or wander, in a rest
Made sweeter for the step upon the grass,
And view the ground's most gentle dimplement

(As if God's finger touched but did not press
In making England) such an up and down
Of verdure,—nothing too much up or down,
A ripple of land; such little hills, the sky
Can stoop to tenderly and the wheatfields
    climb;
Such nooks of valleys lined with orchises,
Fed full of noises by invisible streams;
And open pastures where you scarcely tell
White daisies from white dew,—at intervals
The mythic oaks and elm-trees standing out
Self-poised upon their prodigy of shade,—
I thought my father's land was worthy too
Of being my Shakespeare's.
 . . .
  Breaking into voluble ecstasy
I flattered all the beauteous country round,
As poets use, the skies, the clouds, the fields,
The happy violets hiding from the roads
The primroses run down to, carrying gold;
The tangled hedgerows, where the cows push
    out
Impatient horns and tolerant churning mouths
'Twixt dripping ash-boughs,—hedgerows all
    alive
With birds and gnats and large white but-
    terflies
Which looked as if the May-flower had caught
    life

And palpitated forth upon the wind;
Hills, vales, woods, netted in a silver mist,
Farms, granges, doubled up among the hills;
And cattle grazing in the watered vales,
And cottage-chimneys smoking from the woods,
And cottage-gardens smelling everywhere,
Confused with smell of orchards.
           Elizabeth Barrett Browning.

(Italy Sweet Too!

HAPPY is England! I could be content
    To see no other verdure than its own;
    To feel no other breezes than are blown
Through its tall woods with high romances blent:

Yet do I sometimes feel a languishment
    For skies Italian, and an inward groan
    To sit upon an Alp as on a throne,
And half forget what world or worldling meant.

Happy is England, sweet her artless daughters;
    Enough their simple loveliness for me,
        Enough their whitest arms in silence clinging:

    Yet do I often warmly burn to see
        Beauties of deeper glance, and hear
          their singing,
And float with them about the summer waters.
                      John Keats.)

Beauty Triumphant

(From *Endymion*)

A THING of beauty is a joy for ever:
    Its loveliness increases; it will never
Pass into nothingness; but still will keep
A bower quiet for us, and a sleep
Full of sweet dreams, and health, and quiet breathing.
Therefore, on every morrow, we are wreathing
A flowery band to bind us to the earth,
Spite of despondence, of the inhuman dearth
Of noble natures, of the gloomy days,
Of all the unhealthy and o'er-darken'd ways
Made for our searching: yea, in spite of all,
Some shape of beauty moves away the pall
From our dark spirits. Such the sun, the moon,
Trees old and young, sprouting a shady boon
For simple sheep; and such are daffodils
With the green world they live in; and clear rills

That for themselves a cooling covert make
'Gainst the hot season; the mid forest brake,
Rich with a sprinkling of fair musk-rose
   blooms:
And such too is the grandeur of the dooms
We have imagined for the mighty dead;
All lovely tales that we have heard or read:
An endless fountain of immortal drink,
Pouring unto us from the heaven's brink.
John Keats.

Nature and Humanity

(From *Lines Composed near Tintern Abbey*)

FOR nature then
(The coarser pleasures of my boyish days,
And their glad animal movements all gone by)
To me was all in all.—I cannot paint
What then I was. The sounding cataract
Haunted me like a passion: the tall rock,
The mountain, and the deep and gloomy wood,
Their colours and their forms, were then to me
An appetite; a feeling and a love,
That had no need of a remoter charm,
By thought supplied, nor any interest
Unborrowed from the eye.—That time is past,
And all its aching joys are now no more,
And all its dizzy raptures. Not for this

Faint I, nor mourn nor murmur; other gifts
Have followed; for such loss, I would believe,
Abundant recompense. For I have learned
To look on nature, not as in the hour
Of thoughtless youth; but hearing oftentimes
The still, sad music of humanity,
Nor harsh nor grating, though of ample power
To chasten and subdue. And I have felt
A presence that disturbs me with the joy
Of elevated thoughts: a sense sublime
Of something far more deeply interfused,
Whose dwelling is the light of setting suns,
And the round ocean and the living air,
And the blue sky, and the mind of man:
A motion and a spirit, that impels
All thinking things, all objects of all thought,
And rolls through all things. Therefore am
    I still
A lover of the meadows and the woods,
And mountains; and of all that we behold
From this green earth; of all the mighty world
Of eye and ear, both what they half create,
And what perceive; well pleased to recognise
In nature and the language of the sense,
The anchor of my purest thoughts, the nurse,
The guide, the guardian of my heart, and soul
Of all my moral being.
William Wordsworth

The Rural Pan

(From *Pagan Papers*)

BOTH iron road and level highway are shunned by the rural Pan, who chooses rather to foot it along the sheep-track on the limitless downs or the thwart-leading footpath through copse and spinney, not without pleasant fellowship with feather and fur. Nor does it follow from all this that the god is unsocial. Albeit shy of the company of his more showy brother-deities, he loveth the more unpretentious human kind, especially them that are *adscripti glebæ,* addicted to the kindly soil and to the working thereof: perfect in no way, only simple, cheery sinners. For he is only half a god after all, and the red earth in him is strong. When the pelting storm drives the wayfarers to the sheltering inn, among the little group on bench and settle Pan has been known to appear at times, in homely guise of hedger-and-ditcher or weather-beaten shepherd from the downs. Strange lore and quaint fancy he will then impart, in the musical Wessex or Mercian he has learned to speak so naturally; though it may not be till many a mile away you begin to suspect that you have unwittingly talked with him who

chased the flying Syrinx in Arcady and turned
the tide of fight at Marathon.
                              Kenneth Grahame.

Hymn of Pan ◇ ◇ ◇

FROM the forests and highlands
    We come, we come;
From the river-girt islands,
    Where loud waves are dumb
        Listening to my sweet pipings.

The wind in the reeds and the rushes,
    The bees on the bells of thyme,
The birds on the myrtle bushes,
    The cicale above in the lime,
And the lizards below in the grass,
Were as silent as ever old Tmolus was,
        Listening to my sweet pipings.

Liquid Peneus was flowing,
    And all dark Tempe lay
In Pelion's shadow, outgrowing
    The light of the dying day,
        Speeded by my sweet pipings.
The Sileni, and Sylvans, and Fauns,
    And the Nymphs of the woods and waves,
To the edge of the moist river-lawns,
    And the brink of the dewy caves,
And all that did then attend and follow,

Were silent with love, as you now, Apollo,
    With envy of my sweet pipings.

I sang of the dancing stars,
    I sang of the dædal Earth,
And of Heaven—and the giant wars,
    And Love, and Death, and Birth,—
    And then I changed my pipings,—
Singing how down the vale of Menalus
    I pursued a maiden and clasped a reed:
Gods and men, we are all deluded thus!
    It breaks in our bosom and then we bleed:
All wept, as I think both ye now would,
If envy or age had not frozen your blood,
    At the sorrow of my sweet pipings.
                    Percy Bysshe Shelley.

Callicles' Song

(From *Empedocles on Etna*)

THROUGH the black, rushing
        smoke-bursts,
    Thick breaks the red flame.
All Etna heaves fiercely
    Her forest-clothed frame.

Not here, O Apollo!
Are haunts meet for thee.
But, where Helicon breaks down
In cliff to the sea.

Where the moon-silver'd inlets
Send far their light voice
Up the still vale of Thisbe,
O speed, and rejoice!

On the sward, at the cliff-top,
Lie strewn the white flocks;
On the cliff-side the pigeons
Roost deep in the rocks.

In the moonlight the shepherds
Soft lull'd by the rills,
Lie wrapt in their blankets,
Asleep on the hills.

—What Forms are these coming
So white through the gloom?
What garments out-glistening
The gold-flower'd broom?

What sweet-breathing Presence
Out-perfumes the thyme?
What voices enrapture
The night's balmy prime?—

'Tis Apollo comes leading
His choir, the Nine.
—The Leader is fairest,
But all are divine.

They are lost in the hollows!
They stream up again!
What seeks on this mountain
The glorified train?—

They bathe on this mountain,
In the spring by their road;
Then on to Olympus,
Their endless abode.

—Whose praise do they mention?
Of what is it told?—
What will be for ever;
What was from of old.

First hymn they the Father
Of all things; and then,
The rest of Immortals,
The action of men.

The Day in its hotness,
The strife with the palm;
The Night in its silence,
The Stars in their calm.
     Matthew Arnold.

Bacchus

(From *Endymion*)

AND as I sat, over the light blue hills
    There came a noise of revellers: the rills
Into the wide stream came of purple hue—
    'Twas Bacchus and his crew!
The earnest trumpet spake, and the silver thrills
From kissing cymbals made a merry din—
    'Twas Bacchus and his kin!
Like to a moving vintage down they came,
Crown'd with green leaves, and faces all on flame;
All madly dancing through the pleasant valley,
    To scare thee, Melancholy!

John Keats.

THE LOVER SINGS

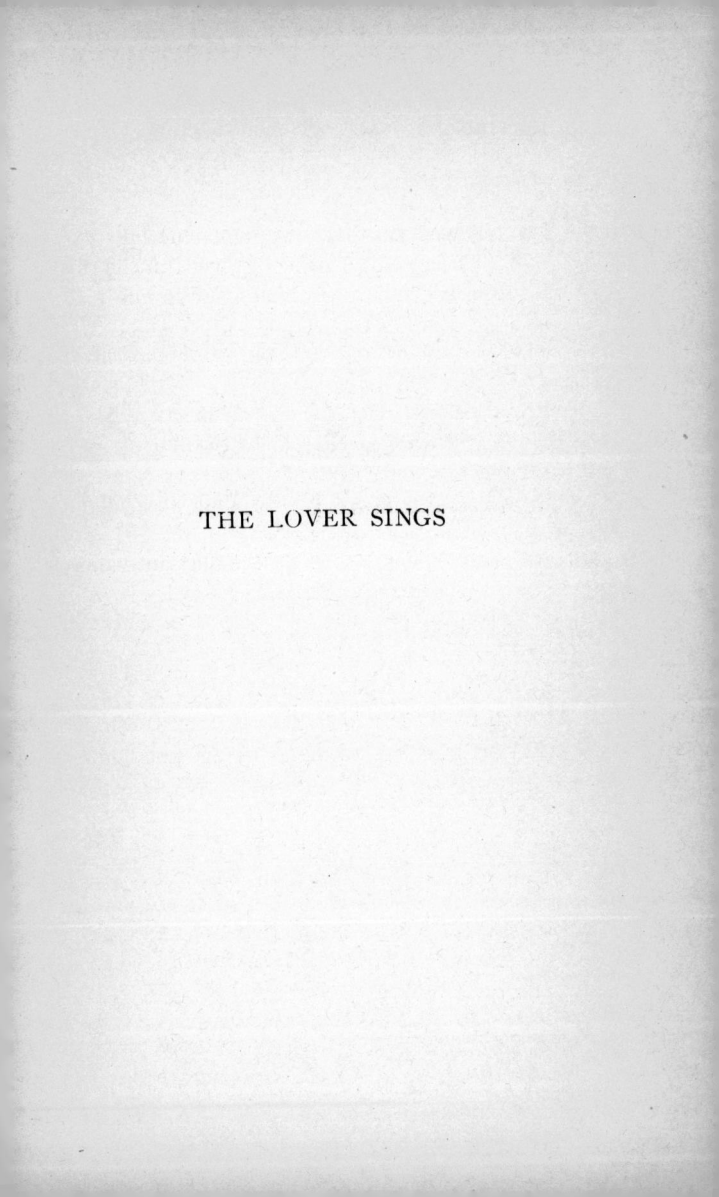

When I walk by myself alone
It doth me good my songs to render.
William Wager

Song

O MISTRESS mine, where are you roaming?
O, stay and hear; your true Love's coming,
That can sing both high and low:
Trip no further, pretty Sweeting;
Journeys end in lovers' meeting,
Every wise man's son doth know.

What is love? 'tis not hereafter;
Present mirth hath present laughter;
What's to come is still unsure:
In delay there lies no plenty:
Then come kiss me, Sweet-and-twenty,
Youth's a stuff will not endure.
William Shakespeare.

Song

LET my voice ring out and over the earth,
Through all the grief and strife,
With a golden joy in a silver mirth:
Thank God for Life!

Let my voice swell out through the great abyss
    To the azure dome above,
With a chord of faith in the harp of bliss:
    Thank God for Love!

Let my voice thrill out beneath and above,
    The whole world through:
O my Love and Life, O my Life and Love,
    Thank God for you!

James Thomson.

Song

OH, like a queen's her happy tread,
    And like a queen's her golden head!
But oh, at last, when all is said,
    Her woman's heart for me!

We wandered where the river gleamed
'Neath oaks that mused and pines that dreamed
A wild thing of the woods she seemed,
    So proud, and pure, and free!

All heaven drew nigh to hear her sing,
When from her lips her soul took wing;
The oaks forgot their pondering,
    The pines their reverie.

And oh, her happy queenly tread,
And oh, her queenly golden head!
But oh, her heart, when all is said,
    Her woman's heart for me!
William Watson.

The Lady of the Lambs

SHE walks—the lady of my delight—
    A shepherdess of sheep.
Her flocks are thoughts. She keeps
    them white;
    She guards them from the steep.
She feeds them on the fragrant height,
    And folds them in for sleep.

She roams maternal hills and bright,
    Dark valleys safe and deep.
Her dreams are innocent at night;
    The chastest stars may peep.
She walks—the lady of my delight—
    A shepherdess of sheep.

She holds her little thoughts in sight,
    Though gay they run and leap.
She is so circumspect and right;
    She has her soul to keep.
She walks—the lady of my delight—
    A shepherdess of sheep.
Alice Meynell.

The Miller's Daughter

IT is the miller's daughter,
   And she is grown so dear, so dear,
That I would be the jewel
   That trembles in her ear:
For hid in ringlets day and night,
I'd touch her neck so warm and bright.

And I would be the girdle
   About her dainty, dainty waist,
And her heart would beat against me,
   In sorrow and in rest:
And I should know if it beat right,
I'd clasp it round so close and tight.

And I would be the necklace,
   And all day long to fall and rise
Upon her balmy bosom,
   With her laughter or her sighs,
And I would lie so light, so light,
I scarce should be unclasp'd at night.
Alfred, Lord Tennyson.

Song

O SWEET delight, O more than human bliss,
With her to live that ever loving is!
To hear her speak whose words are so well placed
That she by them, as they in her are graced!

Those looks to view that feast the viewer's eye,
How blest is he that may so live and die!

Such love as this the Golden Times did know,
When all did reap, yet none took care to sow;
Such love as this an endless summer makes,
And all distate from frail affection takes.
So loved, so blest in my beloved am I:
Which till their eyes do ache, let iron men
    envy!

Thomas Campion.

A Match

IF love were what the rose is,
    And I were like the leaf,
Our lives would grow together
In sad or singing weather,
Blown fields or flowerful closes,
    Green pleasure or grey grief;
If love were what the rose is,
    And I were like the leaf.

If I were what the words are,
    And love were like the tune,
With double sound and single
Delight our lips would mingle,
With kisses glad as birds are
    That get sweet rain at noon;
If I were what the words are
    And love were like the tune.

If you were life, my darling,
   And I your love were death,
We'd shine and snow together
Ere March made sweet the weather
With daffodil and starling
   And hours of fruitful breath;
If you were life, my darling,
   And I your love were death.

If you were thrall to sorrow,
   And I were page to joy,
We'd play for lives and seasons
With loving looks and treasons
And tears of night and morrow
   And laughs of maid and boy,
If you were thrall to sorrow,
   And I were page to joy.

If you were April's lady,
   And I were lord in May,
We'd throw with leaves for hours,
And draw for days with flowers,
Till day like night were shady
   And night were bright like day;
If you were April's lady,
   And I were lord in May.

If you were queen of pleasure,
   And I were king of pain,

We'd hunt down love together,
Pluck out his flying-feather,
And teach his feet a measure,
  And find his mouth a rein;
If you were queen of pleasure,
  And I were king of pain.
            Algernon Charles Swinburne.

She Walks in Beauty

SHE walks in beauty, like the night
  Of cloudless climes and starry skies;
And all that's best of dark and bright
  Meet in her aspect and her eyes:
Thus mellow'd to that tender light
  Which heaven to gaudy day denies.

One shade the more, one ray the less,
  Had half impair'd the nameless grace
Which waves in every raven tress,
  Or softly lightens o'er her face;
Where thoughts serenely sweet express
  How pure, how dear their dwelling-place.

And on that cheek, and o'er that brow,
  So soft, so calm, yet eloquent,
The smiles that win, the tints that glow,
  But tell of days in goodness spent,
A mind at peace with all below,
  A heart wnose love is innocent!
            Lord Byron.

Song   〜 〜 〜 〜

My luve is like a red, red rose
  That's newly sprung in June:
My luve is like the melodie
  That's sweetly played in tune.

As fair thou art, my bonny lass,
  So deep in luve am I:
And I will luve thee still, my dear
  Till a' the seas gang dry.

Till a' the seas gang dry, my dear,
  And the rocks melt wi' the sun:
I will luve thee still, my dear,
  While the sands o' life shall run.

And fare thee weel, my only luve!
  And fare thee weel awhile!
And I will come again, my luve,
  Tho' it were ten thousand mile.
                              Robert Burns.

Song   〜 〜 〜 〜

She is not fair to outward view
  As many maidens be,
Her loveliness I never knew
  Until she smiled on me;
Oh! then I saw her eye was bright,
A well of love, a spring of light.

But now her looks are coy and cold,
  To mine they ne'er reply,
And yet I cease not to behold
  The love-light in her eye:
Her very frowns are fairer far
Than smiles of other maidens are.
                    Hartley Coleridge.

Ballad

It was not in the winter
  Our loving lot was cast:
It was the time of roses,—
  We plucked them as we passed!

That churlish season never frowned
  On early lovers yet!
Oh no—the world was newly crowned
  With flowers, when first we met.

'Twas twilight, and I bade you go,
  But still you held me fast;
It was the time of roses,—
  We plucked them as we passed!

What else could peer my glowing cheek,
  That tears began to stud?
And when I asked the like of Love
  You snatched a damask bud,

And oped it to the dainty core
　　Still glowing to the last:
It was the time of roses,—
　　We plucked them as we passed!
　　　　　　　　Thomas Hood.

Song

GIVE a man a horse he can ride,
　　Give a man a boat he can sail;
And his rank and wealth, his strength and health,
　　On sea nor shore shall fail.

Give a man a pipe he can smoke,
　　Give a man a book he can read;
And his home is bright with a calm delight,
　　Though the room be poor indeed.

Give a man a girl he can love,
　　As I, O my love, love thee;
And his heart is great with the pulse of Fate,
　　At home, on land, on sea.
　　　　　　　　James Thomson.

The Message of the March Wind

(*Fragment*)

FAIR now is the springtide, now earth lies beholding
　　With the eyes of a lover, the face of the sun;

Long lasteth the daylight, and hope is enfolding
    The green-growing acres with increase begun.

Now sweet, sweet it is through the land to be straying
    'Mid the birds and the blossoms and beasts of the field;
Love mingles with love, and no evil is weighing
    On thy heart or mine, where all sorrow is healed.

From township to township, o'er down and by tillage
    Fair, far have we wandered and long was the day;
But now cometh eve at the end of the village,
    Where over the grey wall the church riseth grey.

There is wind in the twilight; in the white road before us
    The straw from the ox-yard is blowing about;
The moon's rim is rising, a star glitters o'er us,
    And the vane on the spire-top is swinging in doubt.

Down there dips the highway, toward the
    bridge crossing over
  The brook that runs on to the Thames and
    the sea.
Draw closer, my sweet, we are lover and lover;
  This eve art thou given to gladness and me.

.   .   .   .

Come back to the inn, love, and the lights and
    the fire,
  And the fiddler's old tune and the shuffling
    of feet;
For there in a while shall be rest and desire,
  And there shall the morrow's uprising be
    sweet.

William Morris.

The Passionate Shepherd to his Love

COME live with me and be my Love,
    And we will all the pleasures prove
That hills and valleys, dale and field,
And all the craggy mountains yield.

There will we sit upon the rocks
And see the shepherds feed their flocks,
By shallow rivers, to whose falls
Melodious birds sing madrigals.

There will I make thee beds of roses
And a thousand fragrant posies,
A cap of flowers, and a kirtle
Embroider'd all with leaves of myrtle.

A gown made of the finest wool,
Which from our pretty lambs we pull,
Fair linéd slippers for the cold,
With buckles of the purest gold.

A belt of straw and ivy buds
With coral clasps and amber studs:
And if these pleasures may thee move,
Come live with me and be my Love.

Thy silver dishes for thy meat
As precious as the gods do eat,
Shall on an ivory table be
Prepared each day for thee and me.

The shepherd swains shall dance and sing
For thy delight each May-morning:
If these delights thy mind may move,
Then live with me and be my Love.
Christopher Marlowe.

Song

THERE is a garden in her face
    Where roses and white lilies blow;
A heavenly paradise is that place,
    Wherein all pleasant fruits do grow;

There cherries grow that none may buy,
Till Cherry-Ripe themselves do cry.

Those cherries fairly do enclose
  Of orient pearl a double row,
Which when her lovely laughter shows,
  They look like rose-buds fill'd with snow;
Yet them no peer nor prince may buy,
Till Cherry-Ripe themselves do cry.

Her eyes like angels watch them still;
  Her brows like bended bows do stand,
Threat'ning with piercing frowns to kill
  All that approach with eye or hand
These sacred cherries to come nigh,
—Till Cherry-Ripe themselves do cry!
Anon.

Her Beauty

WHEN in the chronicle of wasted time
    I see descriptions of the fairest wights,
And beauty making beautiful old rhyme
In praise of ladies dead, and lovely knights;
Then in the blazon of sweet beauty's best
Of hand, of foot, of lip, of eye, of brow,
I see their antique pen would have exprest

Ev'n such a beauty as you master now.
So all their praises are but prophecies
Of this our time, all, you prefiguring;
And for they look'd but with divining eyes,
They had not skill enough your worth to sing:
  For we, which now behold these present days,
  Have eyes to wonder, but lack tongues to praise.

William Shakespeare.

Constancy

WERE I as base as is the lowly plain,
  And you, my Love, as high as heaven above,
Yet should the thoughts of me your humble swain
Ascend to heaven, in honour of my Love.

Were I as high as heaven above the plain,
And you, my Love, as humble and as low
As are the deepest bottoms of the main,
Whereso'er you were, with you my love should go.

Were you the earth, dear Love, and I the skies,
My love should shine on you like to the sun,
And look upon you with ten thousand eyes
Till heaven wax'd blind, and till the world were done.

Whereso'er I am, below, or else above you,
Whereso'er you are, my heart shall truly
    love you.
John Sylvester.

Song

SHE'S somewhere in the sunlight strong,
    Her tears are in the falling rain,
She calls me in the wind's soft song,
    And with the flowers she comes again.

Yon bird is but her messenger,
    The moon is but her silver car;
Yea! sun and moon are sent by her,
    And every wistful waiting star.
Richard Le Gallienne.

SUN AND CLOUD, AND THE
WINDY HILLS

To see the sun to bed and to arise,
Like some hot amourist with glowing eyes,
Bursting the lazy bonds of sleep that bound him
With all his fires and travelling glories round him.
Charles Lamb.

The Sun

(From *The Rhythm of Life*)

THE curious have an insufficient motive for going to the mountains if they do it to see the sunrise. The sun that leaps from a mountain peak is a sun past the dew of his birth; he has walked some way towards the common fires of noon. But on the flat country the uprising is early and fresh, the arc is wide, the career is long. The most distant clouds, converging in the beautiful and little-studied order of cloud perspective (for most painters treat clouds as though they formed perpendicular and not horizontal scenery), are those that gather at the central point of sunrise. On the plain, and there only, can the construction—but that is too vital a word; I should rather say the organism—the unity, the design, of a sky be understood. The light wind that has been moving all night is seen to have not worked at random. It has shepherded some small flocks of cloud afield and folded others. There's husbandry in Heaven. And the order has, or seems to have, the sun for its midst. Not a line, not a curve, but confesses its membership in a design declared from horizon to horizon.

Alice Meynell.

Hymn of Apollo

THE sleepless Hours who watch me as I lie,
   Curtained with star-inwoven tapestries,
From the broad moonlight of the sky,
   Fanning the busy dreams from my dim eyes,
Waken me when their Mother, the grey Dawn,
Tells them that dreams and that the moon is gone.

Then I arise, and, climbing Heaven's blue dome,
   I walk over the mountains and the waves,
Leaving my robe upon the ocean foam;
   My footsteps pave the clouds with fire; the caves
Are filled with my bright presence, and the air
Leaves the green Earth to my embraces bare.

The sunbeams are my shafts, with which I kill
   Deceit, that loves the night and fears the day;

All men who do or even imagine ill
   Fly me, and from the glory of my ray;
Good minds and open actions take new might,
Until diminished by the reign of Night.

I feed the clouds, the rainbows, and the flowers,
   With their ethereal colours; the Moon's globe,
And the pure stars in their eternal bowers,
   Are cinctured with my power as with a robe;
Whatever lamps on Earth or Heaven may shine
Are portions of one power, which is mine.

I stand at noon upon the peak of Heaven;
   Then with unwilling steps I wander down
Into the clouds of the Atlantic even;
   For grief that I depart they weep and frown:
What look is more delightful than the smile
With which I soothe them from the western isle?

I am the eye with which the Universe
   Beholds itself, and knows itself divine;
All harmony of instrument or verse,
   All prophecy, all medicine, are mine,
All light of art or nature;—to my song
Victory and praise in their own right belong.
            Percy Bysshe Shelley.

Youth at the Summit

(From *Pan and the Young Shepherd*)

I GOT up the mountain edge, and from the top saw the world stretch out—corn-lands and forest, the river winding among meadow-flats, and right off, like a hem of the sky, the moving sea, with snatches of foam, and large ships reaching forward, out-bound. And then I thought no more, but my heart leapt to meet the wind, and I ran, and I ran. I felt my legs under me, I felt the wind buffet me, hit me on the cheek; the sun shone, the bees swept past me singing; and I too sang, shouted, World, world, I am coming!

Maurice Hewlett.

Morning on Etna

(From *Empedocles on Etna*)

THE mules, I think, will not be here this
    hour.
They feel the cool wet turf under their feet
By the stream-side, after the dusty lanes
In which they have toil'd all night from
    Catana,
And scarcely will they budge a yard. O Pan,
How gracious is the mountain at this hour!
A thousand times have I been here alone,

Or with the revellers from the mountain towns,
But never on so fair a morn;—the sun
Is shining on the brilliant mountain crests,
And on the highest pines; but further down
Here in the valley is in shade; the sward
Is dark, and on the stream the mist still hangs;
One sees one's footprints crush'd in the wet grass,
One's breath curls in the air; and on these pines
That climb from the stream's edge, the long grey tufts,
Which the goats love, are jewell'd thick with dew.

Matthew Arnold.

The Horizon
From *The Spirit of Place)*

TO mount a hill is to lift with you something lighter and brighter than yourself or than any meaner burden. You lift the world, you raise the horizon; you give a signal for the distance to stand up. It is like the scene in the Vatican when a Cardinal, with his dramatic Italian hands, bids the kneeling groups to arise. He does more than bid them. He lifts them, he gathers them up, far and near, with the upward gesture of both arms; he takes them to their feet with the compulsion of his expressive force. Or it is as when a conductor takes his players to successive heights of music. You summon the sea, you bring the mountains, the distances unfold unlooked-for wings and take an even flight. You are but a man lifting his weight upon the upward road, but as you climb the circle of the world goes up to face you. . . . It is the law whereby the eye and the horizon answer one another that makes the way up a hill so full of universal movement. All the landscape is on pilgrimage. The town gathers itself closer, and its inner harbours literally come to light; the headlands repeat themselves; little cups within the treeless hills open and show their farms. In the sea are many regions. A breeze is at play for a mile or two, and the surface is turned. There are roads and curves in the blue and in the white. Not a step of your journey up the height that has not its replies in the steady motion of land and sea. Things rise together like a flock of many-feathered birds.

Alice Meynell.

The Hill Pantheist

(From *The Story of my Heart*)

MOVING up the sweet short turf, at every step my heart seemed to obtain a wider horizon of feeling; with every inhalation of rich pure air, a deeper desire. The very light of the sun was whiter and more brilliant here. By the time I had reached the summit I had entirely forgotten the petty circumstances and the annoyances of existence. I felt myself, myself. There was an intrenchment on the summit, and going down into the fosse I walked round it slowly to recover breath. On the south-western side there was a spot where the outer bank had partially slipped, leaving a gap. There the view was over a broad plain, beautiful with wheat, and inclosed by a perfect amphitheatre of green hills. Through these hills there was one narrow groove, or pass, southwards, where the white clouds seemed to close in the horizon. Woods hid the scattered hamlets and farmhouses, so that I was quite alone.

I was utterly alone with the sun and the earth. Lying down on the grass, I spoke in my soul to the earth, the sun, the air, and the distant sea far beyond sight. I thought of the earth's firmness—I felt it bear me up; through the grassy couch there came an influence as if I could feel the great earth speaking to me. I thought of the wandering air—its pureness, which is its beauty; the air touched me and gave me something of itself. I spoke to the sea; though so far, in my mind I saw it, green at the rim of the earth and blue in deeper ocean; I desired to have its strength, its mystery and glory. Then I addressed the sun, desiring the soul equivalent of his light and brilliance, his endurance and unwearied race. I turned to the blue heaven over, gazing into its depth, inhaling its exquisite colour and sweetness. The rich blue of the unattainable flower of the sky drew my soul towards it, and there it rested, for pure colour is rest of heart. By all these I prayed; I felt an emotion of the soul beyond all definition; prayer is a puny thing to it, and the word is a rude sign to the feeling, but I know no other.

By the blue heaven, by the rolling sun bursting through untrodden space, a new ocean of ether every day unveiled. By the fresh and wandering air encompassing the world; by the sea sounding on the shore—the green sea white-flecked at the margin and the deep ocean; by the strong earth under me. Then, returning, I prayed by the sweet thyme, whose little flowers I touched with my hand; by the slender grass; by the crumble of dry chalky earth I took up and let fall through my fingers. Touching the crumble of earth, the blade of grass, the thyme flower, breathing the earth-encircling air, thinking of the sea and the sky, holding out my hand for the sunbeams to touch it, prone on the sward in token of deep reverence, thus I prayed that I might touch to the unutterable existence infinitely higher than deity.

Richard Jefferies.

"A Small Sweet Idyll"

(From *The Princess*)

Come down, O maid, from yonder mountain height:
What pleasure lives in height (the shepherd sang)
In height and cold, the splendour of the hills?
But cease to move so near the Heavens, and cease
To glide a sunbeam by the blasted Pine,
To sit a star upon the sparkling spire;
And come, for Love is of the valley, come,
For Love is of the valley, come thou down
And find him; by the happy threshold, he,
Or hand in hand with Plenty in the maize,
Or red with spirted purple of the vats,

Or foxlike in the vine; nor cares to walk
With Death and Morning on the silver horns,
Nor wilt thou snare him in the white ravine,
Nor find him dropt upon the firths of ice,
That huddling slant in furrow-cloven falls
To roll the torrent out of dusky doors:
But follow; let the torrent dance thee down
To find him in the valley; let the wild
Lean-headed Eagles yelp alone, and leave
The monstrous ledges there to slope, and spill
Their thousand wreaths of dangling water-smoke,
That like a broken purpose waste in air:
So waste not thou; but come; for all the vales
Await thee; azure pillars of the hearth
Arise to thee; the children call, and I
Thy shepherd pipe, and sweet is every sound,
Sweeter thy voice, but every sound is sweet;
Myriads of rivulets hurrying thro' the lawn,
The moan of doves in immemorial elms,
And murmuring of innumerable bees.
    Alfred, Lord Tennyson.

The South-West Wind ∽ ∽ ∽

(From *The Colour of Life*)

THE most certain and most conquering of all is the south-west wind. You do not look to the weather-vane to decide what shall be the style of your greeting to his morning. There is no arbitrary rule of courtesy between you and him, and you need no arrow to point to his distinctions, and to indicate to you the right manner of treating such a visitant.

He prepares the dawn. While it is still dark the air is warned of his presence, and before the window was opened he was already in the room. His sun—for the sun is his—rises in a south-west mood, with a bloom on the blue, the grey, or the gold. When the south-west is cold, the cold is his own cold—round, blunt, full, and gradual in its very strength. It is a fresh cold, that comes with an approach, and does not challenge you in the manner of an unauthorised stranger, but instantly gets your leave, and even a welcome to your house of life. He follows your breath in at your throat, and your eyes are open to let him in, even when he is cold. Your blood cools, but does not hide from him.

He has a splendid way with his sky. In his flight, which is that, not of a bird, but of a flock of birds, he flies high and low at once: high with his higher clouds, that keep long in the sight of man, seeming to move slowly; and low with the coloured clouds that breast the hills and are near the tree-tops. These the south-west wind tosses up from his soft horizon, round and successive. They are tinted somewhat like ripe clover-fields, or like hay-fields just before the cutting, when all the grass is in flower, and they are, oftener than all other clouds, in shadow. These low-lying flocks are swift and brief; the wind casts them before him, from the western verge to the eastern.

Alice Meynell.

Ode to the West Wind

O WILD West Wind, thou breath of Autumn's being,
  Thou from whose unseen presence the leaves dead
Are driven like ghosts from an enchanter fleeing,
  Yellow, and black, and pale, and hectic red,
Pestilence-stricken multitudes! O thou
  Who chariotest to their dark wintry bed
The wingèd seeds, where they lie cold and low,
  Each like a corpse within its grave, until
Thine azure sister of the Spring shall blow
  Her clarion o'er the dreaming earth, and fill
(Driving sweet buds like flocks to feed in air)
  With living hues and odours plain and hill;
Wild Spirit which art moving everywhere;
Destroyer and preserver; hear, oh hear!

Thou on whose stream, 'mid the steep sky's commotion,
　Loose clouds like earth's decaying leaves are shed,
Shook from the tangled boughs of heaven and ocean,
　Angels of rain and lightning! there are spread
On the blue surface of thine airy surge,
　Like the bright hair uplifted from the head
Of some fierce Mænad, even from the dim verge
　Of the horizon to the zenith's height,
The locks of the approaching storm. Thou dirge
　Of the dying year, to which this closing night
Will be the dome of a vast sepulchre,
　Vaulted with all thy congregated might
Of vapours, from whose solid atmosphere
Black rain, and fire, and hail, will burst: Oh hear!

Thou who didst waken from his summer dreams
　The blue Mediterranean, where he lay,
Lulled by the coil of his crystalline streams,
　Beside a pumice isle in Baiæ's bay,

And saw in sleep old palaces and towers
   Quivering within the wave's intenser day,
All overgrown with azure moss, and flowers
   So sweet the sense faints picturing them! Thou
For whose path the Atlantic's level powers
   Cleave themselves into chasms, while far below
The sea-blooms and the oozy woods which wear
   The sapless foliage of the ocean know
Thy voice, and suddenly grow grey with fear,
And tremble and despoil themselves: Oh, hear!

If I were a dead leaf thou mightest bear;
   If I were a swift cloud to fly with thee;
A wave to pant beneath thy power, and share
   The impulse of thy strength, only less free
Than thou, O uncontrollable! if even
   I were as in my boyhood, and could be
The comrade of thy wanderings over heaven,
   As then, when to outstrip thy skiey speed
Scarce seemed a vision,—I would ne'er have striven
   As thus with thee in prayer in my sore need.
Oh, lift me as a wave, a leaf, a cloud!
   I fall upon the thorns of life! I bleed!

A heavy weight of hours has chained and bowed
One too like thee—tameless, and swift, and proud.

Make me thy lyre, even as the forest is:
  What if my leaves are falling like its own?
The tumult of thy mighty harmonies
  Will take from both a deep autumnal tone,
Sweet though in sadness. Be thou, Spirit fierce,
  My spirit! Be thou me, impetuous one!
Drive my dead thoughts over the universe,
  Like withered leaves, to quicken a new birth;
And, by the incantation of this verse,
  Scatter, as from an unextinguished hearth
Ashes and sparks, my words among mankind!
  Be through my lips to unawakened earth
The trumpet of a prophecy! O Wind,
If Winter comes, can Spring be far behind?

Percy Bysshe Shelley.

Clouds

(From *The Colour of Life*)

THE cloud, moreover, controls the sun, not merely by keeping the custody of his rays, but by becoming the counsellor of his temper. The cloud veils an angry sun, or, more terribly, lets fly an angry ray, suddenly bright upon tree and tower, with iron-grey storm for a background. Or when anger had but threatened, the cloud reveals him, gentle beyond hope. It makes peace, constantly, just before sunset.

It is in the confidence of the winds, and wears their colours. There is a heavenly game, on south-west wind days, when the clouds are bowled by a breeze from behind the evening. They are round and brilliant, and come leaping up from the horizon for hours. This is a frolic and haphazard sky.

All unlike this is the sky that has a centre, and stands composed about it. As the clouds marshalled the earthly mountains, so the clouds in turn are now ranged. The tops of all the celestial Andes aloft are swept at once by a single ray, warmed with a single colour. Promontory after league-long promontory of a stiller Mediterranean in the sky is called out of mist and grey by the same finger. The cloud-land is very great, but a sunbeam makes all its nations and continents sudden with light.

Alice Meynell.

The Cloud

I BRING fresh showers for the thirsting flowers
    From the seas and the streams;

I bear light shade for the leaves when laid
    In their noonday dreams.
From my wings are shaken the dews that waken
    The sweet buds every one,
When rocked to rest on their Mother's breast,
    As she dances about the sun.
I wield the flail of the lashing hail,
    And whiten the green plains under;
And then again I dissolve it in rain,
    And laugh as I pass in thunder.

I sift the snow on the mountains below,
    And their great pines groan aghast;
And all the night 'tis my pillow white,
    While I sleep in the arms of the Blast.
Sublime on the towers of my skiey bowers
    Lightning my pilot sits;
In a cavern under is fettered the Thunder,
    It struggles and howls at fits.

Over earth and ocean with gentle motion
    This pilot is guiding me,
Lured by the love of the Genii that move
    In the depths of the purple sea;
Over the rills and the crags and the hills,
    Over the lakes and the plains,
Wherever he dream under mountain or stream
    The spirit he loves remains;

And I all the while bask in heaven's blue
      smile,
   Whilst he is dissolving in rains.

The sanguine Sunrise, with his meteor eyes,
      And his burning plumes outspread,
Leaps on the back of my sailing rack,
      When the morning star shines dead:
As on the jag of a mountain-crag
      Which an earthquake rocks and swings
An eagle alit one moment may sit
      In the light of its golden wings.
And, when Sunset may breathe, from the lit sea
      beneath,
      Its ardours of rest and of love,
And the crimson pall of eve may fall
      From the depth of heaven above,
With wings folded I rest on mine airy nest,
      As still as a brooding dove.

That orbèd maiden with white fire laden
      Whom mortals call the Moon
Glides glimmering o'er my fleece-like floor
      By the midnight breezes strewn;
And wherever the beat of her unseen feet,
      Which only the angels hear,
May have broken the woof of my tent's thin
      roof,
      The Stars peep behind her and peer.

And I laugh to see them whirl and flee
    Like a swarm of golden bees,
When I widen the rent in my wind-built tent,—
    Till the calm rivers, lakes, and seas,
Like strips of the sky fallen through me on high,
    Are each paved with the moon and these.

I bind the Sun's throne with a burning zone,
    And the Moon's with a girdle of pearl;
The volcanoes are dim, and the Stars reel and swim,
    When the Whirlwinds my banner unfurl.
From cape to cape, with a bridge-like shape,
    Over a torrent sea,
Sunbeam-proof, I hang like a roof;
    The mountains its columns be.
The triumphal arch through which I march,
    With hurricane, fire, and snow,
When the Powers of the air are chained to my chair,
    Is the million-coloured bow;
The Sphere-fire above its soft colours wove,
    While the moist Earth was laughing below.

I am the daughter of Earth and Water,
    And the nursling of the Sky:

I pass through the pores of the ocean and
   shores;
   I change, but I cannot die.
For after the rain, when with never a stain
   The pavilion of heaven is bare,
And the winds, and sunbeams with their convex gleams
   Build up the blue dome of air,
I silently laugh at my own cenotaph,—
   And out of the caverns of rain,
Like a child from the womb, like a ghost from
   the tomb,
   I arise, and unbuild it again.

Percy Bysshe Shelley.

The Downs ○ ○ ○ ○ ○

O BOLD majestic downs, smooth, fair and
   lonely;
O still solitude, only matched in the skies;
   Perilous in steep places,
   Soft in the level races,
Where sweeping in phantom silence the cloudland flies;
With lovely undulation of fall and rise;
   Entrenched with thickets thorned,
By delicate miniature dainty flowers adorned!

I climb your crown, and lo! a sight surprising
Of sea in front uprising, steep and wide:

    And scattered ships ascending
    To heaven, lost in the blending
Of distant blues, where water and sky divide,
Urging their engines against wind and tide,
    And all so small and slow
They seem to be wearily pointing the way they would go.

The accumulated murmur of soft plashing,
Of waves on rocks dashing, and searching the sands;
    Takes my ear, in the veering
    Baffled wind, as rearing
Upright at the cliff, to the gullies and rifts he stands;
And his conquering surges scour out over the lands;
    While again at the foot of the downs
He masses his strength to recover the topmost crowns.

Robert Bridges.

BIRDS, BLOSSOMS, AND
TREES

God's jocund lyttel fowles.
Old Writer.

And 'tis my faith that every flower
Enjoy the air it breathes.
William Wordsworth.

The holes were already dug, and they set to work. Winterborne's fingers were endowed with a gentle conjuror's touch in spreading the roots of each little tree, resulting in a sort of caress under which the delicate fibres all laid themselves out in their proper directions for growth. He put most of these roots towards the south-west; for, he said, in forty years' time, when some great gale is blowing from that quarter, the trees will require the strongest holdfast on that side to stand against it and not fall.

"How they sigh directly we put 'em upright, though while they are lying down they don't sigh at all," said Mary.

"Do they?" said Giles, "I've never noticed it."

She erected one of the young pines into its hole, and held up her finger; the soft musical breathing instantly set in, which was not to cease night or day till the grown tree should be felled—probably long after the two planters should be felled themselves.

Thomas Hardy ("The Woodlanders").

The Very Birds of the Air

NAY more, the very birds of the air, those that be not hawks, are both so many and so useful and pleasant to mankind, that I must not let them pass without some observations. They both feed and refresh him—feed him with their choice bodies, and refresh him with their heavenly voices. I will not undertake to mention the several kinds of fowl by which this is done, and his curious palate pleased by day, and which with their very excrements afford him a soft lodging at night—these I will pass by; but not those little nimble musicians of the air, that warble forth their curious ditties, with which nature hath furnished them to the shame of art.

As first the lark, when she means to rejoice, to cheer herself and those that hear her; she then quits the earth, and sings as she ascends higher into the air, and having ended her heavenly employment, grows then mute and sad, to think she must descend to the dull earth, which she would not touch, but for necessity.

How do the blackbird and thrassel with their melodious voices bid welcome to the cheerful spring, as in their fixed months warble forth such ditties as no art or instruments can reach to!

Nay, the smaller birds also do the like in their particular seasons, as namely the leverock, the titlark, the little linnet, and the honest robin, that loves mankind both alive and dead.

But the nightingale, another of my airy creatures, breathes such sweet loud music out of her little instrumental throat, that it might make mankind to think miracles are not ceased. He that at midnight, when the very labourer sleeps securely, should hear, as I have very often, the clear airs, the sweet descants, the natural rising and falling, the doubling and redoubling of her voice, might well be lifted above earth, and say, " Lord, what music hast Thou provided for the saints in heaven, when Thou affordest bad men such music on earth?"

Izaak Walton.

The Blackbird

OV al the birds upon the wing
    Between the zunny show'rs o' spring,
Var al the lark, a-swingèn high,
Mid zing sweet ditties to the sky,

An' sparrers, clust'ren roun' the bough,
Mid chatter to the men at plough;
The blackbird, hoppèn down along
The hedge, da zing the gâyest zong.

'Tis sweet, wi' yerly-wakèn eyes
To zee the zun when vust da rise,
Ar, halen underwood an' lops
Vrom new-plesh'd hedges ar vrom copse
To snatch oon's nammet down below
A tree where primruosen da grow,
But ther's noo time the whole da long
Lik' evemen wi' the blackbird's zong.

Var when my work is al a-done
Avore the zettèn o' the zun,
Then blushèn Jian da wa'k along
The hedge to mit me in the drong,
An' stây till al is dim an' dark
Bezides the ashen tree's white bark.
An' al bezides the blackbird's shill
An' runnèn evemen-whissle's still.

How in my buoyhood I did rove
Wi' pryèn eyes along the drove,
Var blackbirds' nestes in the quick-
Set hedges high, an' green, an' thick;
Ar clim' al up, wi' clingèn knees,
Var crows' nestes in swayen trees

109

While frighten'd blackbirds down below
Did chatter o' ther well-know'd foe.

An' we da hear the blackbirds zing
Ther sweetest ditties in the spring,
When nippèn win's na muore da blow
Vrom narthern skies wi' sleet ar snow,
But dreve light doust along between
The cluose leane-hedges, thick an' green;
An' zoo th' blackbird down along
The hedge da zing the gâyest zong.

William Barnes.

Song

PACK, clouds, away, and welcome day,
  With night we banish sorrow;
Sweet air, blow soft, mount, larks, aloft
  To give my love good-morrow!
Wings from the wind to please her mind
  Notes from the lark I'll borrow;
Bird, prune thy wing, nightingale, sing,
  To give my Love good-morrow;
    To give my Love good-morrow
    Notes from them both I'll borrow.

Wake from thy nest, Robin-red-breast,
  Sing, birds, in every furrow;

And from each hill, let music shrill
  Give my fair Love good-morrow!
Blackbird and thrush in every bush,
  Stare, linnet, and cock-sparrow!
You pretty elves, amongst yourselves
  Sing my fair Love good-morrow;
    To give my Love good-morrow
    Sing, birds, in every furrow!
Thomas Heywood.

The Green Linnet

Beneath these fruit-tree boughs that shed
Their snow-white blossoms on my head,
With brightest sunshine round me spread
  Of Spring's unclouded weather,
In this sequester'd nook how sweet
To sit upon my orchard-seat!
And flowers and birds once more to greet,
  My last year's friends together.

One have I mark'd, the happiest guest
In all this covert of the blest:
Hail to Thee, far above the rest
  In joy of voice and pinion!
Thou, Linnet; in thy green array
Presiding Spirit here to-day
Dost lead the revels of the May,
  And this is thy dominion.

While birds, and butterflies, and flowers,
Make all one band of paramours,
Thou, ranging up and down the bowers
Art sole in thy employment;
A Life, a Presence like the air,
Scattering thy gladness without care,
Too blest with any one to pair,
Thyself thy own enjoyment.

Amid yon tuft of hazel trees
That twinkle to the gusty breeze,
Behold him perch'd in ecstasies
Yet seeming still to hover;
There, where the flutter of his wings
Upon his back and body flings
Shadows and sunny glimmerings,
That cover him all over.

My dazzled sight he oft deceives—
A brother of the dancing leaves;
Then flits, and from the cottage-eaves
Pours forth his song in gushes,
As if by that exulting strain
He mock'd and treated with disdain
The voiceless Form he chose to feign
While fluttering in the bushes.

William Wordsworth.

Philomela

HARK! ah, the Nightingale!
  The tawny-throated!
Hark! from that moonlit cedar what a burst!
What triumph! hark!—what pain!

O Wanderer from a Grecian shore,
Still, after many years, in distant lands,
Still nourishing in thy bewilder'd brain
That wild, unquench'd, deep-sunken, old-world pain—
  Say, will it never heal?
And can this fragrant lawn
With its cool trees, and night,
And the sweet, tranquil Thames,
And moonshine, and the dew,
To thy rack'd heart and brain
  Afford no balm?

Dost thou to-night behold
Here, through the moonlight on this English grass,
The unfriendly palace in the Thracian wild?
  Dost thou again peruse
With hot cheeks and sear'd eyes
The too clear web, and thy dumb Sister's shame?

  Dost thou once more assay
Thy flight, and feel come over thee,
Poor Fugitive, the feathery change
Once more, and once more seem to make resound
With love and hate, triumph and agony,
Lone Daulis, and the high Cephissian vale?
  Listen, Eugenia—
How thick the bursts come crowding through the leaves!
  Again—thou hearest!
Eternal Passion!
Eternal Pain!

Matthew Arnold.

Ode to a Nightingale

MY heart aches, and a drowsy numbness pains
 My sense, as though of hemlock I had drunk,
Or emptied some dull opiate to the drains
 One minute past, and Lethe-wards had sunk:
'Tis not through envy of thy happy lot,
 But being too happy in thine happiness,—
  That thou, light-winged Dryad of the trees
   In some melodious plot
Of beechen green, and shadows numberless,
 Singest of summer in full throated ease.

O, for a draught of vintage! that hath been
  Cool'd a long age in the deep-delved earth,
Tasting of Flora and the country green,
  Dance, and Provençal song, and sunburnt mirth!
  O for a beaker full of the warm South,
  Full of the true, the blushful Hippocrene,
    With beaded bubbles winking at the brim,
      And purple-stained mouth;
  That I might drink, and leave the world unseen,
    And with thee fade away into the forest dim:

Fade far away, dissolve, and quite forget
  What thou among the leaves hast never known,
The weariness, the fever, and the fret,
  Here, where men sit and hear each other groan;
Where palsy shakes a few sad, last gray hairs,
  Where youth grows pale, and spectre-thin, and dies;
    Where but to think is to be full of sorrow
      And leaden-eyed despairs,
  Where Beauty cannot keep her lustrous eyes,
    Or new Love pine at them beyond to-morrow.

Away! away! for I will fly to thee,
  Not charioted by Bacchus and his pards,
But on the viewless wings of Poesy,
  Though the dull brain perplexes and retards:
Already with thee! tender is the night,
  And haply the Queen-Moon is on her throne,
    Cluster'd around by all her starry Fays;
      But here there is no light,
  Save what from heaven is with the breezes blown
    Through verdurous glooms and winding mossy ways.

I cannot see what flowers are at my feet,
  Nor what soft incense hangs upon the boughs,
But, in embalmed darkness, guess each sweet
  Wherewith the seasonable month endows
The grass, the thicket, and the fruit-tree wild;
  White hawthorn, and the pastoral eglantine;
    Fast-fading violets cover'd up in leaves;
      And mid-May's eldest child,
  The coming musk-rose, full of dewy wine,
    The murmurous haunt of flies on summer eves.

Darkling I listen; and, for many a time
  I have been half in love with easeful Death,
Call'd him soft names in many a mused rhyme,
  To take into the air my quiet breath;

Now more than ever seems it rich to die,
  To cease upon the midnight with no pain,
    While thou art pouring forth thy soul abroad
      In such an ecstasy!
  Still wouldst thou sing, and I have ears in vain—
  To thy high requiem become a sod.

Thou wast not born for death, immortal Bird!
  No hungry generations tread thee down;
  The voice I hear this passing night was heard
    In ancient days by emperor and clown:
  Perhaps the self-same song that found a path
    Through the sad heart of Ruth, when, sick for home,
      She stood in tears amid the alien corn;
        The same that oft-times hath
    Charm'd magic casements, opening on the foam
    Of perilous seas, in faery lands forlorn.

Forlorn! the very word is like a bell
  To toll me back from thee to my sole self!
Adieu! the fancy cannot cheat so well
  As she is fam'd to do, deceiving elf.
Adieu! adieu! thy plaintive anthem fades
  Past the near meadows, over the still stream,

>   Up the hill-side; and now 'tis buried deep
>   In the next valley-glades:
> Was it a vision, or a waking dream?
>   Fled is that music:—Do I wake or sleep?
>   *John Keats.*

The Daisies

OVER the shoulders and slopes of the dune
  I saw the white daisies go down to the sea,
A host in the sunshine, an army in June,
The people God sends us to set our heart free.

The bobolinks rallied them up from the dell,
The orioles whistled them out of the wood;
And all of their saying was, "Earth, it is well!"
And all of their dancing was, "Life, thou art good!"

Bliss Carman.

To the Daisy

WITH little here to do or see
    Of things that in the great world be,
Sweet Daisy! oft I talk to thee,
    For thou art worthy:

Thou unassuming common-place
Of nature with that homely face,
And yet with something of a grace,
    Which love makes for thee!

Oft do I sit by thee at ease,
And weave a web of similes,
Loose types of things through all degrees,
    Thoughts of thy raising:
And many a fond and idle name
I give to thee, for praise or blame,
As is the humour of the game,
    While I am gazing.

A nun demure, of lowly port;
Or sprightly maiden of love's court,
In thy simplicity the sport
    Of all temptations;
A queen in crown of rubies dress'd
A starveling in a scanty vest;
Are all, as seem to suit thee best,
    Thy appellations.

A little Cyclops, with one eye
Staring to threaten and defy—
That thought comes next—and instantly
    The freak is over.
The shape will vanish, and behold!
A silver shield with boss of gold,
That spreads itself, some fairy bold
    In fight to cover.

I see thee glittering from afar;—
And then thou art a pretty star
Not quite so fair as many are
    In heaven above thee!
Yet like a star, with glittering crest,
Self-poised in air, thou seem'st to rest;
May peace come never to his nest
    Who shall reprove thee!

Sweet flower; for by that name at last,
When all my reveries are past,
I call thee, and to that cleave fast,
    Sweet silent creature!
That breath'st with me in sun and air,
Do thou, as thou art wont, repair
My heart with gladness, and a share
    Of thy meek nature!

                William Wordsworth.

To Daffodils

FAIR Daffodils, we weep to see
    You haste away so soon:
As yet the early-rising sun
    Has not attained his noon.
        Stay, stay,
      Until the hasting day
          Has run
      But to the evensong,
And, having prayed together, we
    Will go with you along.

We have short time to stay as you,
  We have as short a spring,
As quick a growth to meet decay,
  As you, or anything.
      We die,
  As your hours do, and dry
        Away,
  Like to the summer's rain,
Or as the pearls of morning's dew,
  Ne'er to be found again.
                    Robert Herrick.

I Wandered Lonely as a Cloud

I WANDERED lonely as a cloud
    That floats on high o'er vales and hills,
When all at once I saw a crowd,
A host, of golden daffodils;
Beside the lake, beneath the trees,
Fluttering and dancing in the breeze.

Continuous as the stars that shine
And twinkle on the milky way,
They stretched in never-ending line
Along the margin of a bay:
Ten thousand saw I at a glance,
Tossing their heads in sprightly dance.

The waves besides them danced; but they
Out-did the sparkling waves in glee:
A poet could not but be gay,
In such a jocund company:
I gazed—and gazed—but little thought
What wealth the show to me had brought:

For oft, when on my couch I lie
In vacant or in pensive mood,
They flash upon that inward eye
Which is the bliss of solitude;
And then my heart with pleasure fills,
And dances with the daffodils.
William Wordsworth.

Perdita's Gifts

(From *The Winter's Tale*)

PERDITA. Here's flowers for you:
    Hot lavender, mints, savory, marjoram;
The marigold, that goes to bed with the sun,
And with him rises weeping; these are flowers
Of middle summer, and, I think, they are given
To men of middle age: You are very welcome.
  Camillo. I should leave grazing, were I of your flock,
And only live by gazing.

Perdita. Out, alas!
You'd be so lean, that blasts of January
Would blow you through and through.—Now my fairest friend,
I would I had some flowers o' the spring, that might
Become your time of day; and yours; and yours
That wear upon your virgin branches yet
Your maidenheads growing.—O Proserpina,
For the flowers now, that, frighted, thou let'st fall
From Dis's waggon!—daffodils,
That come before the swallow dares, and take
The winds of March with beauty; violets, dim,
But sweeter than the lids of Juno's eyes,
Or Cytherea's breath; pale primroses,
That die unmarried ere they can behold
Bright Phœbus in his strength, a malady
Most incident to maids; bold oxlips, and
The crown-imperial; lilies of all kinds,
The flower-de-luce being one; O, these I lack
To make you garlands of; and, my sweet friend,
To strew him o'er and o'er.
 Florizel. What! like a corse?
 Perdita. No, like a bank, for love to lie and play on:
Not like a corse: or if,—not to be buried,

But quick, and in mine arms. Come, take your
>   flowers:
Methinks I play as I have seen them do
In Whitsun pastorals: sure, this robe of mine
Does change my disposition.
>   *Florizel.* What you do
Still betters what is done. When you speak,
>   sweet,
I'd have you do it ever: when you sing,
I'd have you buy and sell so; so give alms;
Pray so; and, for the ordering your affairs,
To sing them too: when you do dance, I wish
>   you
A wave o' the sea, that you might ever do
Nothing but that; move still, still so, and own
No other function: each your doing,
So singular in each particular,
Crowns what you are doing in the present
>   deeds,
That all your acts are queens.
>   *William Shakespeare.*

To Primroses filled with Morning Dew

WHY do ye weep, sweet babes? can tears
>   Speak grief in you,
>   Who were but born
>   Just as the modest morn
>   Teem'd her refreshing dew?

Alas, you have not known that shower
        That mars a flower,
        Nor felt th' unkind
    Breath of a blasting wind,
    Nor are ye worn with years;
        Or warp'd as we,
    Who think it strange to see
Such pretty flowers, like to orphans young,
To speak by tears, before ye have a tongue.

Speak, whimp'ring younglings, and make known
        The reason why
        Ye droop and weep;
    Is it for want of sleep,
    Or childish lullaby?
Or that ye have not seen as yet
        The violet?
        Or brought a kiss
    From that Sweet-heart, to this?
—No, no, this sorrow shown
        By your tears shed,
    Would have this lecture read,
That things of greatest, so of meanest worth,
Conceived with grief are, and with tears brought forth.

Robert Herrick.

The Woodlands

O SPREAD agen your leaves an' flow'rs,
   Luonesome woodlands! zunny woodlands!
Here underneath the dewy show'rs
   O warm-âir'd spring-time, zunny woodlands.
As when, in drong ar oben groun',
Wi' happy buoyish heart I voun'
The twitt'ren birds a' builden roun'
   Your high-bough'd hedges, zunny woodlands.

Ya gie'd me life, ya gie'd me jày,
   Luonesome woodlands, zunny woodlands;
Ya gie'd me health as in my plây
   I rambled droo ye, zunny woodlands.
Ya gie'd me freedom var to rove
In âiry meäd, ar shiady grove;
Ya gie'd me smilen Fanny's love,
   The best ov al o't, zunny woodlands.

My vust shill skylark whiver'd high,
   Luonesome woodlands, zunny woodlands,
To zing below your deep-blue sky
   An' white spring-clouds, O zunny woodlands,
An' boughs o' trees that oonce stood here,
Wer glossy green the happy year
That gie'd me oon I lov'd so dear
   An' now ha lost, O zunny woodlands.

O let me rove agen unspied,
  Luonesome woodlands, zunny woodlands,
Along your green-bough'd hedges' zide,
  As then I rambled, zunny woodlands.
An' wher the missèn trees oonce stood,
Ar tongues oonce rung among the wood,
My memory shall miake em good,
  Though you've a-lost em, zunny woodlands.

William Barnes.

Tapestry Trees

Oak. I am the Roof-tree and the Keel:
  I bridge the seas for woe and weal.

Fir. High o'er the lordly oak I stand,
And drive him on from land to land.

Ash. I heft my brother's iron bane;
I shaft the spear and build the wain.

Yew. Dark down the windy dale I grow,
The father of the fateful Bow.

Poplar. The war shaft and the milking-bowl
I make, and keep the hay-wain whole.

Olive. The King I bless; the lamps I trim;
In my warm wave do fishes swim.

Apple-tree. I bowed my head to Adam's will;
The cups of toiling men I fill.

Vine. I draw the blood from out the earth;
I store the sun for winter mirth.

Orange-tree. Amidst the greenness of my night
My odorous lamps hang round and bright.

Fig-tree. I who am little among trees
In honey-making mate the bees.

Mulberry-tree. Love's lack hath dyed my berries red:
For Love's attire my leaves are shed.

Pear-tree. High o'er the mead-flowers' hidden feet
I bear aloft my burden sweet.

Bay. Look on my leafy boughs, the Crown
Of living song and dead renown!
William Morris.

The Poet in the Woods

(From *The Task*)

EV'N in the spring and playtime of the year,
  That calls the unwonted villager abroad
With all her little ones, a sportive train,
To gather king-cups in the yellow mead,
And prink their hair with daisies, or to pick
A cheap but wholesome salad from the brook,

These shades are all my own. The tim'rous hare.
Grown so familiar with her frequent guest,
Scarce shuns me; and the stock-dove unalarmed
Sits cooing in the pine-tree, nor suspends
His long love-ditty for my near approach.
Drawn from his refuge in some lonely elm
That age or injury has hollowed deep,
Where on his bed of wool and matted leaves
He has outslept the winter, ventures forth
To frisk awhile, and bask in the warm sun,
The squirrel, flippant, pert, and full of play.
He sees me, and at once, swift as a bird,
Ascends the neighb'ring beech; there whisks his brush,
And perks his ears, and stamps and scolds aloud,
With all the prettiness of feigned alarm,
And anger insignificantly fierce.
William Cowper.

On Solitude ◡ ◡ ◡ ◡

HAIL, old patrician trees, so great and good!
    Hail, ye plebeian underwood!
  Where the poetic birds rejoice,
And for their quiet nests and plenteous food,
  Pay with their grateful voice.

Hail, the poor muse's richest manor seat!
    Ye country houses and retreat,
      Which all the happy gods so love,
That for you oft they quit their bright and great
    Metropolis above.

Here nature does a house for me erect,
    Nature the wisest architect,
      Who those fond artists does despise
That can the fair and living trees neglect,
    Yet the dead timber prize.

Here let me careless and unthoughtful lying,
    Hear the soft winds above me flying
      With all their wanton boughs dispute.
And the more tuneful birds to both replying,
    Nor be myself too mute.

A silver stream shall roll his waters near
    Gilt with the sunbeams here and there,
      On whose enamel'd bank I'll walk,
And see how prettily they smile, and hear
    How prettily they talk.

Ah wretched, and too solitary he
    Who loves not his own company!
      He'll feel the weight of 't many a day
Unless he call in sin or vanity
    To help to bear 't away.

O Solitude, first state of human-kind!
    Which blest remain'd till man did find
    Even his own helper's company.
As soon as two (alas!) together join'd,
    The serpent made up three.

The god himself, through countless ages thee
    His sole companion chose to be,
    Thee, sacred Solitude alone,
Before the branchy head of number's tree
    Sprang from the trunk of one.

Thou (though men think thine an unactive part)
    Dost break and tame th' unruly heart,
    Which else would know no settled pace,
Making it more well manag'd by thy art
    With swiftness and with grace.

Thou the faint beams of reason's scatter'd light,
    Dost like a burning-glass unite,
    Dost multiply the feeble heat,
And fortify the strength, till thou dost bright
    And noble fires beget.

Whilst this hard truth I teach, methinks, I see
    The monster London laugh at me,
    I should at thee too, foolish city,

If it were fit to laugh at misery,
  But thy estate I pity.

Let but thy wicked men from out thee go,
  And all the fools that crowd thee so,
  Even thou who dost thy millions boast,
A village less than Islington wilt grow,
  A solitude almost.

Abraham Cowley.

Song

(Fragment)

UNDER the greenwood tree,
  Who loves to lie with me,
  And tune his merry throat
  Unto the sweet bird's note,
Come hither, come hither, come hither!
  Here shall he see
  No enemy
But winter and rough weather.

Who doth ambition shun,
  And loves to live i' the sun,
  Seeking the food he eats,
  And pleased with what he gets,
Come hither, come hither, come hither,
  Here shall he see
  No enemy
But winter and rough weather.

William Shakespeare.

SUMMER SPORTS AND

PASTIMES

A BOY'S PRAYER

God who created me
  Nimble and light of limb,
In three elements free,
  To run, to ride, to swim;
  Not when the sense is dim,
But now from the heart of joy,
  I would remember Him:
Take the thanks of a boy.

H. C. Beeching.

The Angler's Rest

*C*ORIDON. I will sing a song, if anybody will sing another; else, to be plain with you, I will sing none: I am none of those that sing for meat, but for company: I say, "'Tis merry in hall when men sing all."

Piscator. I'll promise you I'll sing a song that was lately made at my request by Mr. William Basse—one that hath made the choice songs of the "Hunter in his career," and ot "Tom of Bedlam," and many others of note; and this that I will sing is in praise of angling.

Coridon. And then mine shall be the praise of a countryman's life: what will the rest sing of?

Peter. I will promise you I will sing another song in praise of angling to-morrow night; for we will not part till then, but fish to-morrow, and sup together, and the next day every man leave fishing, and fall to his business.

Venator. 'Tis a match; and I will provide you a song or a catch against then, too, which shall give some addition of mirth to the company; for we will be civil and as merry as beggars.

Piscator. 'Tis a match, my masters: let's e'en say grace, and turn to the fire, drink the other cup to wet our whistles, and so sing away all sad thoughts.

Come on, my masters, who begins? I think it is best to draw cuts, and avoid contention.

Peter. It is a match. Look the shortest cut falls to Coridon.

Coridon. Well, then, I will begin, for I hate contention.

Coridon's Song

Oh, the sweet contentment
The countryman doth find!
  Heigh trolollie lollie loe,
  Heigh trolollie lollie lee.
That quiet contemplation
Possesseth all my mind;
  Then care away,
  And wend along with me.

For Courts are full of flattery,
As hath too oft been tried;
  Heigh trolollie lollie loe, etc.

The city full of wantonness,
And both are full of pride:
  Then care away, etc.

But, oh! the honest countryman
Speaks truly from his heart;
  Heigh trolollie lollie loe, etc.
His pride is in his tillage,
His horses and his cart;
  Then care away, etc.

Our clothing is good sheep-skins,
Grey russet for our wives;
  Heigh trolollie lollie loe, etc.
'Tis warmth, and not gay clothing
That doth prolong our lives;
  Then care away, etc.

The ploughman, though he labour hard,
Yet on the holiday,
  Heigh trolollie lollie loe, etc.
No emperor so merrily
Doth pass his time away;
  Then care away, etc.

To recompense our tillage,
The heavens afford us showers;
  Heigh trolollie lollie loe, etc.

And for our sweet refreshments
The earth affords us bowers:
  Then care away, etc.

The cuckoo and the nightingale
Full merrily do sing,
  Heigh trolollie lollie loe, etc.
And with their pleasant roundelays
Bid welcome to the spring;
  Then care away, etc.

This is not half the happiness
The countryman enjoys;
  Heigh trolollie lollie loe, etc.
Though others think they have as much,
Yet he that says so lies;
  Then come away, turn
  Countryman with me.—*Jo. Chalkhill.*

Piscator. Well sung, Coridon! this song was sung with mettle, and it was choicely fitted to the occasion; I shall love you for it as long as I know you. I would you were a brother of the angle: for a companion that is cheerful, and free from swearing and scurrilous discourse, is worth gold. I love such mirth as does not make friends ashamed to look upon one another next morning; nor men that cannot well bear it, to repent the money they spend when they be warmed with drink: and take this for a rule, you may pick out such times and such companions, that you may make yourselves merrier for a little than a great deal of money; for, "'Tis the company and not the charge that makes the feast": and such a companion you prove, I thank you for it.

But I will not compliment you out of the debt that I owe you; and therefore I will begin my song, and wish it may be so well liked.

The Angler's Song

As inward love breeds outward talk,
The hound some praise, and some the hawk;
Some, better pleased with private sport,
Use tennis; some a mistress court:
    But these delights I neither wish
    Nor envy, while I freely fish.

Who hunts, doth oft in danger ride;
Who hawks, lures oft both far and wide;
Who uses games shall often prove
A loser; but who falls in love
    Is fetter'd in fond Cupid's snare:
    My angle breeds me no such care.

Of recreation there is none
So free as fishing is alone;
All other pastimes do no less
Than mind and body both possess;
  My hand alone my work can do
  So I can fish and study too.

I care not, I, to fish in seas—
Fresh rivers best my mind do please,
Whose sweet calm course I contemplate,
And seek in life to imitate:
  In civil bounds I fain would keep,
  And for my past offences weep.

And when the timorous trout I wait
To take, and he devours my bait,
How poor a thing, sometimes I find,
Will captivate a greedy mind;
  And when none bite, I praise the wise,
  Whom vain allurements ne'er surprise.

But yet, though while I fish I fast,
I make good fortune my repast;
And thereunto my friend invite,
In whom I more than that delight;
  Who is more welcome to my dish
  Than to my angle was my fish.

As well content no prize to take,
As use of taken prize to make:
For so our Lord was pleasèd, when
He fishers made fishèrs of men.
   Where (which is in no other game)
   A man may fish and praise His name.

The first men that our Saviour dear
Did choose to wait upon Him here,
Bless'd fishers were, and fish the last
Food was that He on earth did taste:
   I therefore strive to follow those
   Whom He to follow Him hath chose.

Coridon. Well sung, brother! you have paid your debt in good coin. We anglers are all beholden to the good man that made this song: come, hostess, give us more ale and let's drink to him.

Isaak Walton.

The Angler's Virtues

NOW for the inward qualities of the minde; albeit some writers reduce them to twelve heads, which indeed whosoever enjoyeth, cannot chuse but be very compleat in much perfection, yet I must draw them into many more branches. The first, and most especial whereof is, that a skilful angler ought to be a general scoller, and seen in all the Liberal Sciences, as a Grammarian to know how either to write or discourse of his art in true and fitting terms, either without affectation or rudeness. He should have sweetness of speech, to perswade and entice others to delight in an exercise so much laudable. He should have strength of arguments to defend and maintain his profession, against envy or slander.

He should have knowledge in the Sun, Moon, and Stars, that by their aspects he may guesse the seasonableness or unseasonableness of the weather, the breeding of storms, and from what coasts the winds are ever delivered. He should be a good knower of countries, and well used to High-wayes, that by taking the readiest paths to every Lake, Brook and River, his Journies may be more certain and less wearisome. He should have knowledge in proportions of all sorts, whether Circular, Square, or Diametrical, that when he shall be questioned of his diurnal progresses, he may give a Geographical description of the angles and channels of Rivers, how they fall from their heads, and what compasses they fetch in their several windings. He must also have the perfect art of numbering, that in the sounding of Lakes or Rivers, he may know how many foot or inches each severally containeth; and by adding, subtracting or multiplying the same, he may yield the reason of every River's swift or slow current. He should not be unskilful in Musick, that whensoever either melancholy, heaviness of his thoughts, or the perturbations of his own fancies, stirreth up sadness in him, he may remove the same with some godly Hymn or Anthem, of which *David* gives him ample examples.

Gervase Markham.

The Angler's Poesy

AND I do easily believe, that peace and patience, and a calm content, did cohabit in the cheerful heart of Sir Henry Wotton; because I know that when he was beyond seventy years of age he made this description of a part of the present pleasure that possessed him, as he sat quietly in a summer's evening, on a bank, a-fishing. It is a description of the spring; which, because it glided as soft and sweetly from his pen, as that river does at this time, by which it was then made, I shall repeat it unto you:

This day dame Nature seem'd in love;
The lusty sap began to move;
Fresh juice did stir th' embracing vines;
And birds had drawn their valentines.
The jealous trout, that low did lie,
Rose at a well-dissembled fly;
There stood my friend, with patient skill,
Attending of his trembling quill;
Already were the eaves possess'd
With the swift Pilgrim's daubèd nest;
The groves already did rejoice
In Philomel's triumphing voice,
The showers were short, the weather mild,
The morning fresh, the evening smiled.

   Joan takes her neat-rubbed pail, and now
She trips to milk the sand-red cow;
Where, for some sturdy foot-ball swain,
Joan strokes a syllabub or twain.
The fields and gardens were beset
With tulips, crocus, violet;
And now, though late, the modest rose
Did more than half a blush disclose.

   Thus all looks gay and full of cheer,
To welcome the new-livery'd year.

These were the thoughts that then possessed the undisturbed mind of Sir Henry Wotton. Will you hear the wish of another angler, and the commendation of his happy life, which he also sings in verse? viz., Jo. Davors, Esq.:

Let me live harmlessly; and near the brink
   Of Trent or Avon have a dwelling-place,
Where I may see my quill or cork down sink
   With eager bite of perch, or bleak, or dace;
And on the world and my Creator think:
   Whilst some men strive ill-gotten goods t' embrace,
And others spend their time in base excess
Of wine, or worse, in war and wantonness.

Let them that list, these pastimes still pursue,
   And on such pleasing fancies feed their fill;
So I the fields and meadows green may view,
   And daily by fresh rivers walk at will,
Among the daisies and the violets blue,
   Red hyacinth and yellow daffodil,
Purple narcissus like the morning rays,
Pale gander-grass, and azure culverkeys.

I count it higher pleasure to behold
   The stately compass of the lofty sky;
And in the midst thereof, like burning gold,
   The flaming chariot of the world's great eye;
The watery clouds that, in the air up-roll'd,
   With sundry kinds of painted colours fly;

And fair Aurora, lifting up her head,
Still blushing, rise from old Tithonus' bed;

The hills and mountains raisèd from the plains,
  The plains extended level with the ground;
The grounds divided into sundry veins,
  The veins enclos'd with rivers running round;
These rivers making way through nature's chains
  With headlong course into the sea profound;
The raging sea, beneath the valleys low,
Where lakes and rills and rivulets do flow;

The lofty woods, the forests wide and long,
  Adorn'd with leaves and branches fresh and green,
In whose cool bowers the birds, with many a song,
  Do welcome with their choir the summer's queen;
The meadows fair, where Flora's gifts among
  Are intermix'd with verdant grass between;
The silver-scalèd fish that softly swim
Within the sweet brook's crystal watery stream.

All these, and many more of His creation
   That made the heavens, the angler oft doth see;
Taking therein no little delectation,
   To think how strange, how wonderful they be!
Framing thereof an inward contemplation
   To set his heart from other fancies free;
And whilst he looks on these with joyful eye,
His mind is wrapt above the starry sky.

Sir, I am glad my memory has not lost these last verses, because they are somewhat more pleasant and more suitable to May-day than my harsh discourse.

Isaak Walton.

Old Match Days

(From *The Cricketer's Guide*)

THERE was high feasting held on Broad-Halfpenny during the solemnity of one of our grand matches. Oh! it was a heart-stirring sight to witness the multitude forming a complete and dense circle round that noble green. Half the county would be present, and all their hearts with us.—Little Hambledon, pitted against all England, was a proud thought for the Hampshire men. Defeat was glory in such a struggle—Victory, indeed, made us only "a little lower than angels." How those fine brawn-faced fellows of farmers would drink to our success! And then what stuff they had to drink!—Punch!—not your new *Ponche à la Romaine,* or *Ponche à la Groseille,* or your modern cat-lap milk punch—punch bedeviled; but good, unsophisticated, John Bull stuff—stark!—that would stand on end—punch that would make a cat speak! Sixpence a bottle! We had not sixty millions of interest to pay in those days. The ale, too!—not the modern horror under the same name, that drives as many men melancholy-mad as the hypocrites do;—not the beastliness of these days, that will make a fellow's insides like a shaking bog, and as rotten; but barley-corn, such as would put the souls of three butchers into one weaver. Ale that would flare like turpentine—genuine Boniface!—This immortal viand (for it was more than liquor) was vended at twopence per pint. The immeasurable villany of our vintners would, with their march of intellect (if ever they could get such a brewing), drive a pint of it out into a gallon. Then the quantity the fellows would eat! Two or three of them would strike dismay into a round of beef.

They could no more have pecked in that style than they could have flown, had the infernal black stream (that type of Acheron!) which soddens the carcass of a Londoner, been the fertilizer of their clay. There would this company, consisting most likely of some thousands, remain patiently and anxiously watching every turn of fate in the game, as if the event had been the meeting of two armies to decide their liberty. And whenever a Hambledon man made a good hit, worth four or five runs, you would hear the deep mouths of the whole multitude baying away in pure Hampshire—" Go hard!—go hard!—*Tich* and turn!—*tich* and turn!" To the honour of my countrymen, let me bear testimony upon this occasion also, as I have already done upon others. Although their provinciality in general, and personal partialities individually, were naturally interested in behalf of the Hambledon men, I cannot call to recollection an instance of their wilfully stopping a ball that had been hit out among them by one of our opponents. Like *true* Englishmen, they would give an enemy fair play. How strongly are all those scenes, of fifty years by-gone, painted in my memory!—and the smell of that ale comes upon me as freshly as the new May flowers.

John Nyren.

The Cricket Ball Sings

LEATHER—the heart o' me, leather—the rind o' me,
  O but the soul of me's other than that!
Else, should I thrill as I do so exultingly
  Climbing the air from the thick o' the bat?
Leather—the heart o' me: ay, but in verity
  Kindred I claim with the sun in the sky.
Heroes, bow all to the little red ball,
  And bow to my brother ball blazing on high.

  Pour on us torrents of light, good Sun,
    Shine in the hearts of my cricketers, shine;
  Fill them with gladness and might, good Sun,
    Touch them with glory, O Brother of mine,
      Brother of mine,
      Brother of mine!
  We are the lords of them, Brother and Mate,
  I but a little ball, thou but a Great!

Give me the bowler whose fingers embracing me
  Tingle and throb with the joy of the game,

One who can laugh at a smack to the
 boundary,
 Single of purpose and steady of aim.
That is the man for me: striving in sympathy,
 Ours is a fellowship sure to prevail.
Willow must fall in the end to the ball—
 See, like a tiger I leap for the bail.

Give me the fieldsman whose eyes never stray
 from me,
 Eager to clutch me, a roebuck in pace:
Perish the unalert, perish the "buttery,"
 Perish the laggard I strip in the race.
Grand is the ecstasy soaring triumphantly,
 Holding the gaze of the meadow is grand,
Grandest of all to the soul of the ball
 Is the finishing grip of the honest brown
 hand.

Give me the batsman who squanders his force
 on me,
 Crowding the strength of his soul in a
 stroke;
Perish the muff and the little tin Shrewsbury,
 Meanly contented to potter and poke.
He who would pleasure me, he must do
 doughtily,—
 Bruises and buffetings stir me like wine.

Giants, come all, do your worst with the ball,
  Sooner or later you're mine, sirs, you're mine.

  Pour on us torrents of light, good Sun,
    Shine in the hearts of my Cricketers, shine,
  Fill them with gladness and might, good Sun
    Touch them with glory, O Brother of mine,
      Brother of mine,
      Brother of mine!
We are the Lords of them, Brother and Mate:
I but a little ball, thou but a Great.

E. V. Lucas.

Going Down Hill on a Bicycle

A Boy's Song

WITH lifted feet, hands still,
    I am poised, and down the hill
Dart, with heedful mind;
The air goes by in a wind.

Swifter and yet more swift,
Till the heart, with a mighty lift,
Makes the lungs laugh, the throat cry—
"O bird, see; see, bird, I fly.

"Is this, is this your joy,
O bird, then I, though a boy,
For a golden moment share
Your feathery life in air!"

Say, heart, is there aught like this
In a world that is full of bliss?
'Tis more than skating, bound
Steel-shod to the level ground.

Speed slackens now, I float
Awhile in my airy boat;
Till when the wheels scarce crawl,
My feet to the pedals fall.

Alas, that the longest hill
Must end in a vale; but still,
Who climbs with toil, wheresoe'er,
Shall find wings waiting there.
H. C. Beeching.

REFRESHMENT AND THE INN

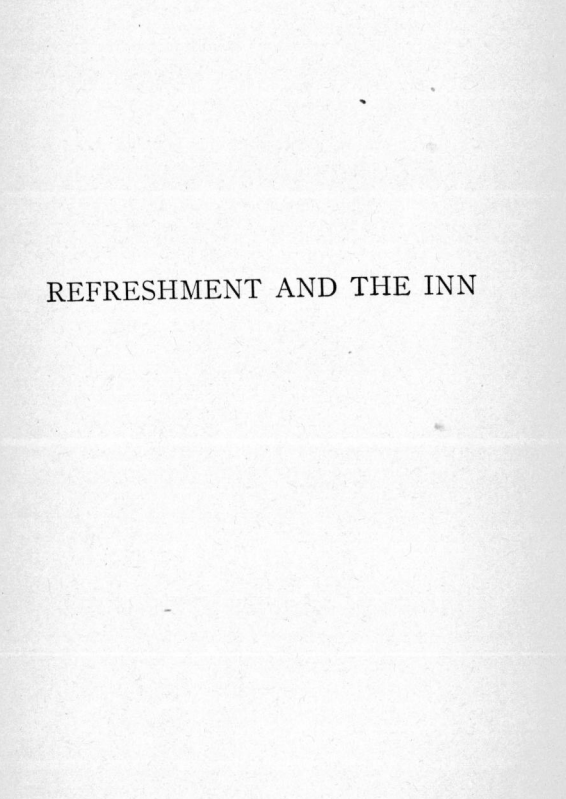

But hark! a sound is stealing on my ear—
  A soft and silvery sound—I know it well.
Its tinkling tells me that a time is near
  Precious to me—it is the Dinner Bell.
O blessed Bell! thou bringest beef and beer,
  Thou bringest good things more than tongue may tell!
Seared is, of course, my heart—but unsubdued
Is, and shall be, my appetite for food.
                                C. S. Calverley.

If I were King, my pipe should be Premier.
                                W. E. Henley.

The Respect due to Hunger

(From *On Going a Journey*)

I GRANT there is one subject on which it is pleasant to talk on a journey; and that is, what one shall have for supper when we get to our inn at night. The open air improves this sort of conversation or friendly altercation, by setting a keener edge on appetite. Every mile of the road heightens the flavour of the viands we expect at the end of it. How fine it is to enter some old town, walled and turreted, just at the approach of nightfall, or to come to some straggling village, with the lights streaming through the surrounding gloom; and then after inquiring for the best entertainment that the place affords, to "take one's ease at one's inn!" These eventful moments in our lives' history are too precious, too full of solid, heartfelt happiness to be frittered and dribbled away in imperfect sympathy. I would have them all to myself, and drain them to the last drop: they will do to talk of or to write about afterwards. What a delicate speculation it is, after drinking whole goblets of tea,

"The cups that cheer, but not inebriate,"

and letting the fumes ascend into the brain, to sit considering what we shall have for supper—eggs and a rasher, a rabbit smothered in onions, or an excellent veal cutlet! Sancho in such a situation once fixed upon cow-heel; and his choice, though he could not help it, is not to be disparaged. Then, in the intervals of pictured scenery and Shandean contemplation, to catch the preparation and the stir in the kitchen—*Procul, O procul, este profani!* These hours are sacred to silence and to musing, to be treasured up in the memory, and to feed the source of smiling thoughts hereafter. I would not waste them in idle talk.

William Hazlitt.

The Power of Malt
(*Fragment*)

WHY, if 'tis dancing you would be,
There's brisker pipes than poetry.
Say, for what were hop-yards meant,
Or why was Burton built on Trent?

Oh, many a peer of England brews
Livelier liquor than the Muse,
And malt does more than Milton can
To justify God's ways to man.
Ale, man, ale's the stuff to drink
For fellows whom it hurts to think:
Look into the pewter pot
To see the world as the world's not.
                              A. E. Housman.

In Praise of Ale

WHEN as the Chilehe Rocko blowes
    And Winter tells a heavy tale
When Pyes and Dawes and Rookes and Crows
Sit cursing of the frosts and snowes;
        Then give me Ale.

Ale in a Saxon Rumken then,
    Such as will make Grim Malkin prate;
Rouseth up valour in all men
Quickens the Poet's wit and pen,
        Despiseth fate.

Ale that the absent battle fights,
    And frames the march of Swedish drum,
Disputes the Prince's lawes and rights,
And what is past and what's to come
        Tells mortal wights.

Ale that the Plowman's heart up keeps
  And equals it with Tyrants' thrones,
That wipes the eye that over weeps,
And lulls in dainty and sure sleeps
    His wearied bones.

Grandchild of Ceres, Burley's daughter,
  Wine's emulous neighbour though but stale,
Innobling all the Nymphs of water
And filling each man's heart with laughter—
    Ha! Ha! give me ale!
                                Old Song.

The Meditative Tankard

(From *Polonius*)

THE parapet balustrade round the roof of Castle Ashby, in Northamptonshire, is carved into the letters, " Nisi Dominus custodiat domum, frustra vigilat qui custodit eam." This is not amiss to decipher as you come up the long avenue some summer or autumn day, and to moralise upon afterwards at the little " Rose and Crown " at Yardley, if such good

Homebrewed be there as used to be before I knew I was to die.

Edward FitzGerald.

Two Recipes

I. The Best Marrow-Bone Pye

AFTER you have mixt the crusts of the best sort for pasts, and raised the coffin in such a manner as you please; you shall first in the bottome thereof lay a course of marrow of beef, mixt with currants; then upon it a lay of the soals of artichokes, after they have been boyled and are divided from the thistle; then cover them with marrow, currants, and great raisins, the stones pickt out; then lay a course of potatoes cut in thick slices, after they have been boiled soft, and are clean pilled; then cover them with marrow, currants, great raisins, sugar, and cinnamon; then lay a layer of candied eringo roots mixt very thick with the slices of dates; then cover it with marrow, currants, great raisins, sugar, cinnamon, and dates, with a few Damask prunes, and so bake it; and after it is bak't, pour into it, as long as it will receive it, white wine, rosewater, sugar, and cinnamon and vinegar mixt together, and candy all the cover with rosewater and sugar only, and so set it into the oven a little, and serve it forth.

II. An Excellent Sallet

TAKE a good quantity of blancht almonds, and with your shredding knife cut them grossly; then take as many raisins of the sun clean washt, and the stones pickt out, as many figs shred like the almonds, as many capers, twice as many olives, and as many currants as of all the rest, clean washt, a good handfull of the small tender leaves of red sage and spinage; mixe all these well together with good store of sugar, and lay them in the bottome of a great dish; then put unto them vinegar and oyl, and scrape more sugar over all; then take oranges and lemmons, and paring away the outward pills, cut them into thin slices, then with those slices cover the sallet all over, which done, take the fine thin leaf of the red cole flower, and with them cover the oranges and lemmons all over; then over those red leaves lay another course of old olives, and the slices of well pickled cucumbers, together with the very inward heart of cabbage-lettuce cut into slices; then adorn the sides of the dish, and the top of the sallet, with more slices of lemmons and oranges, and so serve it up.

Gervase Markham.

The Humble Feast

NOW for a more humble Feast, or an ordinary proportion which any good man may keep in his family, for the entertainment of his true and worthy friends, it must hold limitation with his provision and the season of the year; for Summer affords what Winter wants, and Winter is Master of that which Summer can but with difficulty have. It is good then for him that intends to Feast to set down the full number of his full dishes, that is, dishes of meat that are of substance, and not empty, or for shew; and of these sixteen is a good proportion for one course unto one messe, as thus, for example: First, a shield of Brawn with mustard, Secondly, a boyl'd Capon, Thirdly, a boyl'd piece of Beef, Fourthly, a chine of Beef rosted, Fifthly, a Neat's tongue rosted, Sixthly, a Pig rosted, Seventhly, Chewets bak'd, Eighthly, a Goose rosted, Ninthly, a Swan rosted, Tenthly, a Turkey rosted, the Eleventh, a Haunch of

Venison rosted, the Twelfth, a Pasty of Venison, the Thirteenth, a Kid with a pudding in the belly, the Fourteenth, an Olive-pye, the Fifteenth, a couple of Capons, the Sixteenth, a Custard or Dousets. Now to these full dishes may be added Sallets, Fricases, Quelque choses, and devised paste, as many dishes more, which make the full service no less than two and thirty dishes, which is as much as can conveniently stand on one Table, and in one mess; and after this manner you may proportion both your second and third Course, holding fulness in one half of the dishes, and shew in the other, which will be both frugall in the spender, contentment to the guests, and much pleasure and delight to the beholders.

Gervase Markham.

Salvation Yeo's Testimony to Tobacco

(From *Westward Ho!*)

AH sir, no lie, but a blessed truth, as I can tell, who have ere now gone in the strength of this weed three days and nights without eating; and therefore, sir, the Indians always carry it with them on their war-parties: and no wonder; for when all things were made none was made better than this: to be a lone man's companion, a bachelor's friend, a hungry man's food, a sad man's cordial, a wakeful man's sleep, and a chilly man's fire, sir; while for stanching of wounds, purging of rheum, and settling of the stomach, there's no herb like unto it under the canopy of heaven.

Charles Kingsley.

GARDEN AND ORCHARD

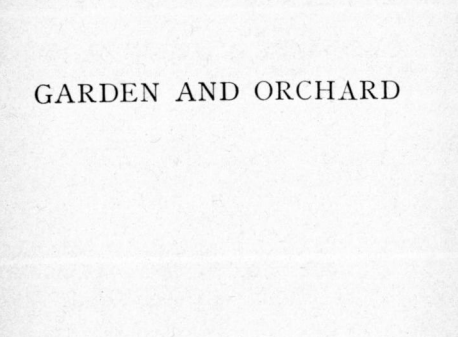

"THE IDLE LIFE I LEAD"

The idle life I lead
Is like a pleasant sleep,
Wherein I rest and heed
The dreams that by me sweep.

And still of all my dreams
In turn so swiftly past,
Each in its fancy seems
A nobler than the last.

And every eve I say
Noting my step in bliss,
That I have known no day,
In all my life like this.

Robert Bridges.

My Garden 〜　〜　〜　〜

A GARDEN is a lovesome thing, God wot!
    Rose plot,
  Fringed pool,
Ferned grot—
    The veriest school
    Of peace; and yet the fool
Contends that God is not—
Not God! in gardens! when the eve is cool?
    Nay, but I have a sign:
    'Tis very sure God walks in mine.
                Thomas Edward Brown.

A Garden Song 〜　〜　〜　〜

HERE, in this sequestered close
    Bloom the hyacinth and rose;
Here beside the modest stock
Flaunts the flaring hollyhock;
Here, without a pang, one sees
Ranks, conditions, and degrees.

All the seasons run their race
In this quiet resting-place;

Peach, and apricot, and fig
Here will ripen, and grow big;
Here is store and overplus,—
More had not Alcinous!

Here, in alleys cool and green,
Far ahead the thrush is seen;
Here along the southern wall
Keeps the bee his festival;
All is quiet else—afar
Sounds of toil and turmoil are.

Here be shadows large and long;
Here be spaces meet for song;
Grant, O garden-god, that I,
Now that none profane is nigh,—
Now that mood and moment please,
Find the fair Pierides!
Austin Dobson.

The Garden

HOW vainly men themselves amaze,
  To win the palm, the oak, or bays,
And their incessant labours see
Crowned from some single herb, or tree,
Whose short and narrow-verged shade
Does prudently their toils upbraid,
While all the flowers and trees do close
To weave the garlands of repose!

Fair Quiet, have I found thee here,
And Innocence, thy sister dear?
Mistaken long, I sought you then
In busy companies of men.
Your sacred plants, if here below,
Only among the plants will grow;
Society is all but rude
To this delicious solitude.

No white nor red was ever seen
So amorous as this lovely green.
Fond lovers, cruel as their flame,
Cut in these trees their mistress' name:
Little, alas! they know or heed,
How far these beauties her exceed!
Fair trees! where'er your barks I wound,
No name shall but your own be found.

When we have run our passion's heat,
Love hither makes his best retreat.
The gods, who mortal beauty chase,
Still in a tree did end their race;
Apollo hunted Daphne so,
Only that she might laurel grow;
And Pan did after Syrinx speed,
Not as a nymph, but for a reed.

What wondrous life is this I lead!
Ripe apples drop about my head;

The luscious clusters of a vine
Upon my mouth do crush their wine;
The nectarine, and curious peach,
Into my hands themselves do reach;
Stumbling on melons, as I pass,
Ensnared with flowers, I fall on grass.

Meanwhile the mind, from pleasure less,
Withdraws into its happiness;—
The mind, that ocean where each kind
Does straight its own resemblance find;
Yet it creates, transcending these,
Far other worlds, and other seas,
Annihilating all that's made
To a green thought in a green shade.

Here at the fountain's sliding foot,
Or at some fruit-tree's mossy root,
Casting the body's vest aside,
My soul into the boughs does glide:
There, like a bird, it sits and sings,
Then whets and claps its silver wings,
And, till prepared for longer flight,
Waves in its plumes the various light.

Such was that happy garden-state,
While man there walked without a mate:
After a place so pure and sweet,
What other help could yet be meet!

But 'twas beyond a mortal's share
To wander solitary there:
Two paradises are in one,
To live in paradise alone.

How well the skilful gardener drew
Of flowers, and herbs, this dial new,
Where, from above, the milder sun
Does through a fragrant zodiac run,
And, as it works, the industrious bee
Computes its time as well as we!
How could such sweet and wholesome hours
Be reckoned but with herbs and flowers?
Andrew Marvell.

Of Gardens

AND because the breath of flowers is far sweeter in the air, where it comes and goes, like the warbling of music, than in the hand, therefore nothing is more fit for that delight, than to know what be the flowers and plants that do best perfume the air. . . . That which above all others yields the sweetest smell in the air, is the violet; especially the white double violet, which comes twice a year, about the middle of April, and about

Bartholomew-tide. Next to that is the musk rose; then the strawberry leaves dying, with a most excellent cordial smell; then the flower of the vines—it is a little dust, like the dust of a bent, which grows upon the cluster, in the first coming forth; then sweet-brier; then wallflowers, which are very delightful, to be set under a parlour, or lower chamber window; then pinks and gilliflowers, especially the matted pink and clove gilliflower; then the flowers of the lime-tree; then the honey-suckles, so they be somewhat afar off. Of bean-flowers I speak not, because they are field-flowers; but those which perfume the air most delightfully, not passed by as the rest, but being trodden upon and crushed, are three; that is, burnet, wild thyme, and water mints. Therefore you are to set whole alleys of them, to have the pleasure when you walk or tread.

Francis Bacon.

Of an Orchard

GOOD is an Orchard, the Saint saith,
    To meditate on life and death,
With a cool well, a hive of bees,
A hermit's grot below the trees.

Good is an Orchard: very good,
Though one should wear no monkish hood
Right good, when Spring awakes her flute,
And good in yellowing time of fruit.

Very good in the grass to lie
And see the network 'gainst the sky,
A living lace of blue and green,
And boughs that let the gold between.

The bees are types of souls that dwell
With honey in a quiet cell;
The ripe fruit figures goldenly
The soul's perfection in God's eye.

Prayer and praise in a country home,
Honey and fruit: a man might come,
Fed on such meats, to walk abroad,
And in his Orchard talk with God.
        Katharine Tynan Hinkson.

The Apple

(From *Winter Sunshine*)

THE boy is indeed the true apple-eater, and is not to be questioned how he came by the fruit with which his pockets are filled. It belongs to him, and he may steal it if it cannot be had in any other way. His own juicy flesh craves the juicy flesh of the apple. Sap draws sap. His fruit-eating has little reference to the state of his appetite. Whether he be full of meat or empty of meat he wants the apple just the same. Before meal or after meal it never comes amiss. The farm-boy munches apples all day long. He has nests of them in the hay-mow, mellowing, to which he makes frequent visits. . . .

The apple is indeed the fruit of youth. As we grow old we crave apples less. It is an ominous sign. When you are ashamed to be seen eating them on the street; when you can carry them in your pocket and your hand not constantly find its way to them; when your neighbour has apples and you have none, and you make no nocturnal visits to his orchard; when your lunch-basket is without them and you can pass a winter's night by the fireside with no thought of the fruit at your elbow, then be assured you are no longer a boy, either in heart or years.

John Burroughs.

MUSIC BENEATH A BRANCH

He [the poet] doth not only show you the way, but giveth so sweet a prospect into the way, as will entice any man to enter into it; nay, he doth, as if your journey should lie through a fair vineyard, at the very first give you a cluster of grapes, that full of that taste you may long to pass farther. . . . He cometh to you with words set in delightful proportion . . . and with a tale, forsooth, he cometh unto you; with a tale which holdeth children from play, and old men from the chimney-corner.

Sir Philip Sidney.

The Scholar-Gipsy

Go, for they call you, Shepherd, from the hill;
    Go, Shepherd, and untie the wattled cotes!
No longer leave thy wistful flock unfed,
Nor let thy bawling fellows rack their throats,
    Nor the cropp'd grasses shoot another head.
      But when the fields are still,
And the tired men and dogs all gone to rest,
    And only the white sheep are sometimes seen
    Cross and recross the strips of moon-blanch'd green;
Come, Shepherd, and again begin the quest.

Here, where the reaper was at work of late,
    In this high field's dark corner, where he leaves
    His coat, his basket, and his earthen cruse,
And in the sun all morning binds the sheaves,
    Then here, at noon, comes back his stores to use;
      Here will I sit and wait,
While to my ear from uplands far away
    The bleating of the folded flocks is borne;
    With distant cries of reapers in the corn—
All the live murmur of a summer's day.

Screen'd is this nook o'er the high, half-reap'd field,
  And here till sun-down, Shepherd! will I be.
    Through the thick corn the scarlet poppies peep
    And round green roots and yellowing stalks I see;
      Pale blue convolvulus in tendrils creep;
        And air-swept lindens yield
Their scent, and rustle down their perfum'd showers
    Of bloom on the bent grass where I am laid,
    And bower me from the August sun with shade;
  And the eye travels down to Oxford's towers:

And near me on the grass lies Glanvil's book—
  Come, let me read the oft-read tale again,
    The story of that Oxford scholar poor
  Of pregnant parts and quick inventive brain,
    Who, tir'd of knocking at Preferment's door,
      One summer morn forsook
    His friends, and went to learn the Gipsy-lore,
      And roam'd the world with that wild brotherhood,

And came, as most men deem'd, to little good,
But came to Oxford and his friends no more.

But once, years after, in the country lanes,
  Two scholars, whom at college erst he knew,
  Met him, and of his way of life enquir'd;
Whereat he answer'd, that the Gypsy crew,
  His mates, had arts to rule as they desir'd
    The workings of men's brains;
And they can bind them to what thoughts they will:
  "And I," he said, "the secret of their art,
  When fully learn'd, will to the world impart;
But it needs happy moments for this skill."

This said, he left them, and return'd no more,
  But rumours hung about the country-side,
  That the lost Scholar long was seen to stray,
  Seen by rare glimpses, pensive and tongue-tied,
  In hat of antique shape, and cloak of grey,
    The same the Gipsies wore.
Shepherds had met him on the Hurst in spring;

At some lone alehouse in the Berkshire moors,
On the warm ingle-bench, the smock-frock'd boors
Had found him seated at their entering,

But, mid their drink and clatter, he would fly:
And I myself seem half to know thy looks,
And put the shepherds, Wanderer! on thy trace;
And boys who in lone wheat fields scare the rooks
I ask if thou hast pass'd their quiet place;
Or in my boat I lie
Moor'd to the cool bank in the summer heats,
Mid wide grass meadows which the sunshine fills,
And watch the warm, green-muffled Cumner hills,
And wonder if thou haunt'st their shy retreats.

For most, I know, thou lov'st retired ground!
Thee, at the ferry, Oxford riders blithe,
Returning home on summer-nights, have met
Crossing the stripling Thames at Bab-lock-hithe,
Trailing in the cool stream thy fingers wet,

As the slow punt swings round;
And leaning backwards in a pensive dream,
And fostering in thy lap a heap of flowers
Pluck'd in shy fields and distant Woodland bowers,
And thine eyes resting on the moonlit stream.

And then they land, and thou art seen no more.
Maidens, who from the distant hamlets come
To dance around the Fyfield elm in May,
Oft through the darkening fields have seen thee roam,
Or cross a stile into the public way.
Oft thou hast given them store
Of flowers—the frail-leaf'd, white anemone—
Dark bluebells drench'd with dews of summer eves—
And purple orchises with spotted leaves—
But none hath words she can report of thee.

And, above Godstow Bridge, when hay-time's here
In June, and many a scythe in sunshine flames,
Men who through those wide fields of breezy grass
Where black-wing'd swallows haunt the glittering Thames,

To bathe in the abandon'd lasher pass,
　Have often pass'd thee near
Sitting upon the river bank o'ergrown;
　Mark'd thine outlandish garb, thy figure spare,
　Thy dark vague eyes, and soft abstracted air;
But, when they came from bathing, thou wert gone!

At some lone homestead in the Cumner hills,
　Where at her open door the housewife darns,
　　Thou hast been seen, or hanging on a gate
　To watch the threshers in the mossy barns.
　Children, who early range these slopes and late
　　For cresses from the rills,
Have known thee watching, all an April day,
　The springing pastures and the feeding kine;
　And mark'd thee, when the stars come out and shine,
Through the long dewy grass move slow away.

In Autumn, on the skirts of Bagley Wood—
　Where most the Gipsies by the turf-edg'd way

Pitch their smok'd tents, and every bush
  you see
With scarlet patches tagg'd and shreds of
  grey,
  Above the forest-ground call'd Thessaly—
  The blackbird, picking food,
Sees thee, nor stops his meal, nor fears at all;
  So often has he known thee past him
    stray,
  Rapt, twirling in thy hand a wither'd
    spray,
And waiting for the spark from Heaven to
  fall.

And once, in winter, on the causeway chill
  Where home through flooded fields foot-
    travellers go,
    Have I not pass'd thee on the wooden
      bridge,
  Wrapt in thy cloak and battling with the
    snow,
    Thy face towards Hinksey and its wintry
      ridge?
    And thou hast climb'd the hill,
  And gain'd the white brow of the Cumner
    range;
    Turn'd once to watch, while thick the
      snow-flakes fall,

The line of festal light in Christ-Church hall—
Then sought thy straw in some sequester'd grange.

But what—I dream! Two hundred years are flown
Since first thy story ran through Oxford halls,
And the grave Glanvil did the tale inscribe
That thou wert wander'd from the studious walls
To learn strange arts, and join a Gypsy-tribe;
And thou from earth art gone
Long since, and in some quiet churchyard laid—
Some country-nook, where o'er thy unknown grave
Tall grasses and white flowering nettles wave,
Under a dark, red-fruited yew-tree's shade.

—No, no, thou hast not felt the lapse of hours!
For what wears out the life of mortal men?
'Tis that from change to change their being rolls;

'Tis that repeated shocks, again, again,
  Exhaust the energy of strongest souls
    And numb the elastic powers.
Till having us'd our nerves with bliss and teen,
  And tir'd upon a thousand schemes our wit,
  To the just-pausing Genius we remit
Our worn-out life, and are—what we have been.

Thou hast not liv'd, why should'st thou perish, so?
  Thou hadst *one* aim, *one* business, *one* desire;
    Else wert thou long since number'd with the dead!
Else hadst thou spent, like other men, thy fire!
  The generations of thy peers are fled,
    And we ourselves shall go;
But thou possessest an immortal lot,
  And we imagine thee exempt from age
  And living as thou liv'st on Glanvil's page,
Because thou hadst—what we, alas! have not.

For early didst thou leave the world, with powers
Fresh, undiverted to the world without,

    Firm to their mark, not spent on other things;
Free from the sick fatigue, the languid doubt,
    Which much to have tried, in much been baffled, brings.
        O Life unlike to ours!
Who fluctuate idly without term or scope,
    Of whom each strives, nor knows for what he strives,
    And each half lives a hundred different lives;
Who wait like thee, but not, like thee, in hope.

Thou waitest for the spark from heaven! and we
    Light half-believers of our casual creeds,
    Who never deeply felt, nor clearly will'd,
Whose insight never has borne fruit in deeds,
    Whose vague resolves never have been fulfill'd;
        For whom each year we see
Breeds new beginnings, disappointments new;
    Who hesitate and falter life away,
    And lose to-morrow the ground won to-day—
Ah! do not we, Wanderer! await it too?

Yes, we await it, but it still delays,
   And then we suffer! and amongst us One,
     Who most has suffer'd, takes dejectedly
His seat upon the intellectual throne;
     And all his store of sad experience he
        Lays bare of wretched days;
Tells us his misery's birth and growth and signs,
   And how the dying spark of hope was fed,
   And how the breast was sooth'd, and how the head,
And all his hourly varied anodynes.

This for our wisest: and we others pine,
   And wish the long unhappy dream would end,
     And waive all claim to bliss, and try to bear
With close-lipp'd Patience for our only friend,
     Sad Patience, too near neighbour to Despair—
        But none has hope like thine!
Thou through the fields and through the woods dost stray,
   Roaming the country-side, a truant boy,
   Nursing thy project in unclouded joy,
And every doubt long blown by time away.

O born in days when wits were fresh and
    clear,
  And life ran gaily as the sparkling Thames;
    Before this strange disease of modern life,
  With its sick hurry, its divided aims,
    Its head o'ertax'd, its palsied hearts, was
        rife—
      Fly hence, our contact fear!
    Still fly, plunge deeper in the bowering
        wood!
      Averse, as Dido did with gesture stern
      From her false friend's approach in Hades
        turn,
    Wave us away, and keep thy solitude!

Still nursing the unconquerable hope,
  Still clutching the inviolable shade,
    With a free, onward impulse brushing
        through,
    By night, the silver'd branches of the
        glade—
      Far on the forest skirts, where none pursue,
        On some mild pastoral slope
      Emerge, and resting on the moonlit pales
      Freshen thy flowers as in former years
      With dew, or listen with enchanted ears,
    From the dark dingles, to the nightingales!

But fly our paths, our feverish contact fly!
  For strong the infection of our mental strife,
    Which, though it gives no bliss, yet spoils
        for rest;
  And we should win thee from thy own fair
        life,
    Like us distracted, and like us unblest.
      Soon, soon thy cheer would die,
  Thy hopes grow timorous, and unfix'd thy
        powers,
    And thy clear aims be cross and shifting
        made;
    And then thy glad perennial youth would
        fade,
  Fade, and grow old at last, and die like ours.

Then fly our greetings, fly our speech and
        smiles!
  —As some grave Tyrian trader from the
        sea,
  Descried at sunrise an emerging prow
  Lifting the cool-hair'd creepers stealthily,
    The fringes of a southward-facing brow
      Among the Aegean isles;
  And saw the merry Grecian coaster come,
    Freighted with amber grapes, and Chian
        wine,

   Green, bursting figs, and tunnies steep'd
      in brine;
And knew the intruders on his ancient
    home,
The young light-hearted Masters of the
    waves—
   And snatch'd his rudder, and shook out
      more sail;
    And day and night held on indignantly
   O'er the blue Midland waters with the gale,
   Betwixt the Syrtes and soft Sicily,
      To where the Atlantic raves
   Outside the Western Straits; and unbent
      sails
    There, where down cloudy cliffs, through
      sheets of foam,
   Shy traffickers, the dark Iberians come;
And on the beach undid his corded bales.
              Matthew Arnold.

L'Allegro

HENCE, loathéd Melancholy,
   Of Cerberus and blackest Midnight
     born
In Stygian cave forlorn,
'Mongst horrid shapes, and shrieks, and
   sights unholy!

Find out some uncouth cell
  Where brooding Darkness spreads his jealous wings
And the night raven sings;
  There, under ebon shades and low-browed rocks
As ragged as thy locks,
  In dark Cimmerian desert ever dwell.
  But come, thou goddess fair and free,
In heaven yclept Euphrosyne,
And by men heart-easing Mirth,
Whom lovely Venus, at a birth
With two sister Graces more,
To ivy-crowned Bacchus bore:
Or whether (as some sager sing)
The frolic wind that breathes the spring,
Zephyr, with Aurora playing
As he met her once a-Maying,
There, on beds of violets blue
And fresh-blown roses washed in dew,
Filled her with thee, a daughter fair,
So buxom, blithe, and debonair.
  Haste thee, nymph, and bring with thee
Jest, and youthful Jollity,
Quips, and Cranks, and wanton Wiles,
Nods, and Becks, and wreathéd Smiles,
Such as hang on Hebe's cheek
And love to live in dimple sleek;
Sport that wrinkled Care derides,

And Laughter holding both his sides.
Come, and trip it, as you go
On the light fantastic toe;
And in thy right hand lead with thee
The mountain nymph, sweet Liberty;
And, if I give thee honour due,
Mirth, admit me of thy crew,
To live with her, and live with thee,
In unreprovéd pleasures free:—
   To hear the lark begin his flight,
And, singing, startle the dull night,
From his watch-tower in the skies,
Till the dappled dawn doth rise;
Then to come, in spite of sorrow,
And at my window bid good-morrow,
Through the sweet-briar, or the vine,
Or the twisted eglantine,
While the cock, with lively din,
Scatters the rear of darkness thin,
And to the stack, or the barn-door,
Stoutly struts his dames before;
Oft listening how the hounds and horn
Cheerly rouse the slumbering morn,
From the side of some hoar hill,
Through the high wood echoing shrill;
Sometime walking, not unseen,
By hedge-row elms, on hillocks green,
Right against the eastern gate
Where the great sun begins his state

Robed in flames and amber light,
The clouds in thousand liveries dight,
While the ploughman, near at hand,
Whistles o'er the furrowed land,
And the milkmaid singeth blithe,
And the mower whets his scythe,
And every shepherd tells his tale
Under the hawthorn in the dale.

  Straight mine eye hath caught new pleasures,
Whilst the landscape round it measures:
Russet lawns, and fallows gray,
Where the nibbling flocks do stray;
Mountains, on whose barren breast
The labouring clouds do often rest;
Meadows trim, with daisies pied,
Shallow brooks, and rivers wide;
Towers and battlements it sees
Bosomed high in tufted trees,
Where, perhaps, some beauty lies,
The cynosure of neighbouring eyes.

  Hard by, a cottage chimney smokes
From betwixt two agéd oaks,
Where Corydon and Thyrsis met,
Are at their savoury dinner set
Of herbs, and other country messes,
Which the neat-handed Phillis dresses,
And then in haste her bower she leaves,
With Thestylis to bind the sheaves;

Or, if the earlier season lead,
To the tanned haycock in the mead.
  Sometimes, with secure delight,
The upland hamlets will invite,
When the merry bells ring round,
And the jocund rebecks sound
To many a youth and many a maid
Dancing in the checkered shade,
And young and old come forth to play
On a sunshine holyday,
Till the livelong daylight fail:
Then to the spicy nut-brown ale,
With stories told of many a feat:
How fairy Mab the junkets eat;
She was pinched, and pulled, she said;
And he, by friar's lantern led,
Tells how the drudging goblin sweat
To earn his cream-bowl duly set,
When, in one night, ere glimpse of morn,
His shadowy flail hath threshed the corn
That ten day-labourers could not end;
Then lies him down the lubber fiend,
And, stretched out all the chimney's length,
Basks at the fire his hairy strength,
And crop-full, out of doors he flings,
Ere the first cock his matin rings.
Thus done the tales, to bed they creep,
By whispering winds soon lulled asleep.
  Towered cities please us then,

And the busy hum of men,
Where throngs of knights and barons bold,
In weeds of peace, high triumphs hold,
With store of ladies, whose bright eyes
Rain influence, and judge the prize
Of wit or arms, while both contend
To win her grace whom all commend.
There let Hymen oft appear
In saffron robe, with taper clear,
And pomp, and feast, and revelry,
With mask and antique pageantry;
Such sights as youthful poets dream
On summer eves by haunted stream.
Then to the well-trod stage anon,
If Jonson's learnéd sock be on,
Or sweetest Shakespeare, Fancy's child,
Warble his native wood-notes wild,
And ever, against eating cares,
Lap me in soft Lydian airs
Married to immortal verse,
Such as the meeting soul may pierce
In notes with many a winding bout
Of linkéd sweetness long drawn out,
With wanton heed and giddy cunning,
The melting voice through mazes running,
Untwisting all the chains that tie
The hidden soul of harmony;
That Orpheus' self may heave his head,
From golden slumber on a bed

Of heaped Elysian flowers, and hear
Such strains as would have won the ear
Of Pluto to have quite set free
His half-regained Eurydice.
These delights if thou canst give,
Mirth, with thee I mean to live.

John Milton.

Song

Rarely, rarely comest thou,
   Spirit of Delight!
Wherefore hast thou left me now
   Many a day and night?
Many a weary night and day
'Tis since thou art fled away.

How shall ever one like me
   Win thee back again?
With the joyous and the free
   Thou wilt scoff at pain.
Spirit false! thou hast forgot
All but those who need thee not.

As a lizard with the shade
   Of a trembling leaf,
Thou with sorrow art dismayed;
   Even the sighs of grief

Reproach thee, that thou art not near,
And reproach thou wilt not hear.

Let me set my mournful ditty
　To a merry measure:
Thou wilt never come for pity,
　Thou wilt come for pleasure;
Pity then will cut away
Those cruel wings, and thou wilt stay.

I love all that thou lovest,
　Spirit of Delight!
The fresh Earth in new leaves dressed,
　And the starry night,
Autumn evening, and the morn
When the golden mists are born.

I love snow, and all the forms
　Of the radiant frost;
I love waves, and winds, and storms—
　Everything almost
Which is Nature's, and may be
Untainted by man's misery.

I love tranquil solitude,
　And such society
As is quiet, wise, and good;
　Between thee and me
What difference? But thou dost possess
The things I seek, not love them less.

I love Love—though he has wings,
    And like light can flee;
But above all other things,
    Spirit, I love thee—
Thou art love and life! Oh, come,
Make once more my heart thy home!
                Percy Bysshe Shelley.

In the Highlands

IN the highlands, in the country places,
    Where the old plain men have rosy faces,
And the young fair maidens
Quiet eyes;
Where essential silence cheers and blesses,
And for ever in the hill-recesses
Her more lovely music
Broods and dies.

O to mount again where erst I haunted;
Where the old red hills are bird-enchanted,
And the low green meadows
Bright with sward;
And when even dies, the million-tinted,
And the night has come, and planets glinted,
Lo, the valley hollow
Lamp-bestarred!

O to dream, O to awake and wander
There, and with delight to take and render
Through the trance of silence
Quiet breath;
Lo! for there, among the flowers and grasses,
Only the mightier movement sounds and passes;
Only winds and rivers,
Life and Death.
Robert Louis Stevenson.

The Solitary Reaper

BEHOLD her, single in the field,
Yon solitary Highland Lass!
Reaping and singing by herself;
Stop here, or gently pass!
Alone she cuts and binds the grain,
And sings a melancholy strain;
O listen! for the Vale profound
Is overflowing with the sound.

No Nightingale did ever chaunt
More welcome notes to weary bands
Of travellers in some shady haunt
Among Arabian sands:
A voice so thrilling ne'er was heard
In spring-time from a Cuckoo-bird,
Breaking the silence of the seas
Among the farthest Hebrides.

Will no one tell me what she sings?—
Perhaps the plaintive numbers flow
For old, unhappy, far-off things,
And battles long ago:
Or is it some more humble lay
Familiar matter of to-day?
Some natural sorrow, loss, or pain,
That has been, and may be again?

Whate'er the theme, the Maiden sang
As if her song could have no ending;
I saw her singing at her work,
And o'er the sickle bending;—
I listened, motionless and still;
And, as I mounted up the hill,
The music in my heart I bore,
Long after it was heard no more.
William Wordsworth.

Ruth

SHE stood breast high among the corn,
  Clasped by the golden light of morn,
Like the sweetheart of the sun,
Who many a glowing kiss had won.

On her cheek an autumn flush,
Deeply ripened;—such a blush
In the midst of brown was born,
Like red poppies grown with corn.

Round her eyes her tresses fell,
Which were blackest none could tell,
But long lashes veiled a light,
That had else been all too bright.

And her hat, with shady brim,
Made her tressy forehead dim;
Thus she stood amid the stooks,
Praising God with sweetest looks:

Sure, I said, Heav'n did not mean,
Where I reap thou shouldst but glean;
Lay thy sheaf adown and come,
Share my harvest and my home.
Thomas Hood.

Cadmus and Harmonia

(From *Empedocles on Etna*)

FAR, far, from here,
   The Adriatic breaks in a warm bay
Among the green Illyrian hills; and there
The sunshine in the happy glens is fair,
And by the sea, and in the brakes.
The grass is cool, the sea-side air
Buoyant and fresh, the mountain flowers
More virginal and sweet than ours.

And there, they say, two bright and aged Snakes,
Who once were Cadmus and Harmonia,
Bask in the glens or on the warm sea-shore,
In breathless quiet, after all their ills.
Nor do they see their country, nor the place
Where the Sphinx lived among the frowning hills,
Nor the unhappy palace of their race,
Nor Thebes, nor the Ismenus, any more.

There those two live, far in the Illyrian brakes.
They had stay'd long enough to see,
In Thebes, the billow of calamity
Over their own dear children roll'd,
Curse upon curse, pang upon pang,
For years, they sitting helpless in their home;
A grey old man and woman, yet of old
The gods had to their marriage come,
And at the banquet all the Muses sang.

Therefore they did not end their days
In sight of blood; but were rapt, far away,
To where the west wind plays,
And murmurs of the Adriatic come
To those untrodden mountain-lawns; and there

Placed safely in changed forms, the Pair
Wholly forget their first sad life, and home,
And all that Theban woe, and stray
For ever, through the glens, placid and dumb.
> *Matthew Arnold.*

Ode on a Grecian Urn

THOU still unravish'd bride of quietness,
  Thou foster-child of silence and slow time,
Sylvan historian, who canst thus express
  A flowery tale more sweetly than our rhyme:
What leaf-fring'd legend haunts about thy shape
  Of deities or mortals, or of both,
    In Tempé or the dales of Arcady?
What men or gods are these? What maidens loth?
  What mad pursuit? What struggles to escape?
    What pipes and timbrels? What wild ecstasy?

Heard melodies are sweet, but those unheard
  Are sweeter; therefore, ye soft pipes, play on;
Not to the sensual ear, but, more endear'd,
  Pipe to the spirit ditties of no tone:

Fair youth, beneath the trees, thou canst not leave
  Thy song, nor ever can those trees be bare;
    Bold Lover, never, never canst thou kiss,
Though winning near the goal—yet, do not grieve;
    She cannot fade, though thou hast not thy bliss,
      For ever wilt thou love, and she be fair!

Ah, happy, happy boughs! that cannot shed
  Your leaves, nor ever bid the Spring adieu
And, happy melodist, unweariéd
  For ever piping songs for ever new;
More happy love! more happy, happy love!
  For ever warm and still to be enjoy'd,
    For ever panting, and for ever young;
All breathing human passion far above,
  That leaves a heart high-sorrowful and cloy'd,
    A burning forehead, and a parching tongue.

Who are these coming to the sacrifice?
  To what green altar, O mysterious priest,
Lead'st thou that heifer lowing at the skies,
  And all her silken flanks with garlands drest?

What little town by river or sea shore,
  Or mountain-built with peaceful citadel,
    Is emptied of this folk, this pious morn?
And, little town, thy streets for evermore
  Will silent be; and not a soul to tell
    Why thou art desolate, can e'er return.

O Attic shape! Fair attitude! with brede
Of marble men and maidens overwrought,
With forest branches and the trodden weed;
  Thou, silent form, dost tease us out of thought
As doth eternity: Cold Pastoral!
  When old age shall this generation waste,
    Thou shalt remain, in midst of other woe
Than ours, a friend to man, to whom thou say'st,
  "Beauty is truth, truth beauty,"—that is all
    Ye know on earth, and all ye need to know.

John Keats.

The Lotus-Eaters

"COURAGE!" he said, and pointed toward the land,
"This mounting wave will roll us shoreward soon."
In the afternoon they came unto a land

In which it seemed always afternoon.
All round the coast the languid air did swoon,
Breathing like one that hath a weary dream.
Full-faced above the valley stood the moon;
And like a downward smoke, the slender stream
Along the cliff to fall and pause and fall did seem.

A land of streams! some, like a downward smoke,
Slow-dropping veils of thinnest lawn, did go;
And some thro' wavering lights and shadows broke,
Rolling a slumbrous sheet of foam below.
They saw the gleaming river seaward flow
From the inner land; far off, three mountain-tops,
Three silent pinnacles of aged snow,
Stood sunset-flush'd: and, dew'd with showery drops,
Up-clomb the shadowy pine above the woven copse.

The charmed sunset linger'd low adown
In the red West: thro' mountain clefts the dale
Was seen far inland, and the yellow down
Border'd with palm, and many a winding vale
And meadow, set with slender galingale;

A land where all things always seem'd the same!
And round about the keel with faces pale,
Dark faces pale against that rosy flame,
The mild-eyed melancholy Lotus-eaters came.

Branches they bore of that enchanted stem,
Laden with flower and fruit, whereof they gave
To each, but whoso did receive of them,
And taste, to him the gushing of the wave
Far far away did seem to mourn and rave
On alien shores; and if his fellow spake,
His voice was thin, as voices from the grave;
And deep-asleep he seem'd, yet all awake,
And music in his ears his beating heart did make.

They sat them down upon the yellow sand,
Between the sun and moon upon the shore;
And sweet it was to dream of Fatherland,
Of child, and wife, and slave; but evermore
Most weary seem'd the sea, weary the oar,
Weary the wandering fields of barren foam.
Then some one said, "We will return no more";
And all at once they sang, "Our island home
Is far beyond the wave; we will no longer roam."

Alfred, Lord Tennyson.

The Forsaken Merman

COME, dear children, let us away;
    Down and away below.
Now my brothers call from the bay;
Now the great winds shorewards blow;
Now the salt tides seawards flow;
Now the wild white horses play,
Champ and chafe and toss in the spray.
        Children dear, let us away!
            This way, this way!

Call her once before you go.
        Call once yet.
In a voice that she will know:
        "Margaret; Margaret!"
Children's voices should be dear
(Call once more) to a mother's ear:
Children's voices, wild with pain.
        Surely she will come again.
Call her once, and come away.
        This way, this way.
"Mother dear, we cannot stay."
The wild white horses foam and fret.
        Margaret! Margaret!

Come, dear children, come away down.
        Call no more.
One last look at the white-walled town,
And the little grey church on the windy shore.

> Then come down.
>
> She will not come though you call all day.
>
> > Come away, come away.

Children dear, was it yesterday
We heard the sweet bells over the bay?
> In the caverns where we lay,
> > Through the surf and through the swell,
The far-off sound of a silver bell?
Sand-strewn caverns, cool and deep,
Where the winds are all asleep;
Where the spent lights quiver and gleam;
Where the salt weed sways in the stream;
Where the sea-beasts, ranged all round,
Feed in the ooze of their pasture-ground;
Where the sea-snakes coil and twine,
Dry their mail and bask in the brine;
Where great whales come sailing by,
Sail and sail, with unshut eye,
Round the world for ever and aye?
> When did music come this way?
> Children dear, was it yesterday?

Children dear, was it yesterday
(Call yet once) that she went away?
Once she sate with you and me,
On a red gold throne in the heart of the sea,
> And the youngest sate on her knee.

She combed its bright hair, and she tended it well,
When down swung the sound of the far-off bell.
She sighed, she looked up through the clear green sea.
She said: "I must go, for my kinsfolk pray
In the little grey church on the shore to-day.
'Twill be Easter-time in the world—ah me!
And I lose my poor soul, Merman, here with thee."
I said: "Go up, dear heart, through the waves;
Say thy prayer, and come back to the kind sea-caves!"
 She smiled, she went up through the surf in the bay.
  Children dear, was it yesterday?
  Children dear, were we long alone?
"The sea grows stormy, the little ones moan;
Long prayers," I said, "in the world they say.
Come," I said, and we rose through the surf in the bay.
We went up the beach, by the sandy down
Where the sea-stocks bloom, to the white-walled town.
Through the narrow paved streets, where all was still,
To the little grey church on the windy hill.

From the church came a murmur of folk at
   their prayers,
But we stood without in the cold blowing airs.

We climbed on the graves, on the stones, worn
   with rains,
And we gazed up the aisle through the small
   leaded panes.
   She sate by the pillar; we saw her clear:
   "Margaret, hist! come quick, we are
      here!
   Dear heart," I said, "we are long alone.
   The sea grows stormy, the little ones
      moan."
But, ah, she gave me never a look,
For her eyes were sealed to the holy book.
   "Loud prays the priest; shut stands
      the door."
Come away, children, call no more!
Come away, come down, call no more!

   Down, down, down.
   Down to the depths of the sea.
She sits at her wheel in the humming town,
   Singing most joyfully.
Hark what she sings: "O joy, O joy,
For the humming street, and the child with its
   toy.
For the priest, and the bell, and the holy well.

  For the wheel where I spun,
   And the blessed light of the sun!"
  And so she sings her fill,
  Singing most joyfully,
  Till the shuttle drops from her hand,
   And the whizzing wheel stands still.
She steals to the window, and looks at the sand;

  And over the sand at the sea;
  And her eyes are set in a stare;
  And anon there breaks a sigh,
  And anon there drops a tear
  From a sorrow-clouded eye,
  And a heart sorrow-laden,
   A long, long sigh
For the cold strange eyes of a little Mer‑
  maiden
   And the gleam of her golden hair.

  Come away, away, children.
  Come, children, come down.
  The hoarse wind blows colder;
  Lights shine in the town.
  She will start from her slumber
  When gusts shake the door;
  She will hear the winds howling,
  Will hear the waves roar.
  We shall see, while above us
  The waves roar and whirl,

A ceiling of amber,
A pavement of pearl.
Singing: "Here came a mortal,
But faithless was she.
And alone dwell for ever
The kings of the sea."

But children, at midnight,
When soft the winds blow,
When clear falls the moonlight;
When spring-tides are low:
When sweet airs come seaward
From heaths starred with broom;
And high rocks throw mildly
On the blanched sands a gloom:
Up the still, glistening beaches,
Up the creeks we will hie;
Over banks of bright seaweed
The ebb-tide leaves dry.
We will gaze, from the sand-hills,
At the white, sleeping town;
At the church on the hill-side—
    And then come back down,
Singing: "There dwells a loved one,
But cruel is she.
She left lonely for ever
The kings of the sea."
Matthew Arnold.

Kubla Khan

IN Xanadu did Kubla Khan
  A stately pleasure-dome decree:
Where Alph, the sacred river, ran
Through caverns measureless to man
  Down to a sunless sea.
So twice five miles of fertile ground
With walls and towers were girdled round:
And there were gardens bright with sinuous rills
Where blossomed many an incense-bearing tree;
And here were forests ancient as the hills,
Enfolding sunny spots of greenery.

  But O! that deep romantic chasm which slanted
Down the green hill athwart a cedarn cover!
A savage place! as holy and enchanted
As e'er beneath a waning moon was haunted
By woman wailing for her demon-lover!
And from this chasm, with ceaseless turmoil seething,
As if this Earth in fast thick pants were breathing,
A mighty fountain momently was forced:
Amid whose swift half-intermitted burst
Huge fragments vaulted like rebounding hail,

Or chaffy grain beneath the thresher's flail:
And 'mid these dancing rocks at once and ever
It flung up momently the sacred river.
Five miles meandering with a mazy motion
Through wood and dale the sacred river ran,
Then reached the caverns measureless to man,
And sank in tumult to a lifeless ocean:
And 'mid this tumult Kubla heard from far
Ancestral voices prophesying war!

    The shadow of the dome of pleasure
    Floated midway on the waves;
    Where was heard the mingled measure
    From the fountain and the caves.
It was a miracle of rare device,
A sunny pleasure-dome with caves of ice!
    A damsel with a dulcimer
    In a vision once I saw:
    It was an Abyssinian maid,
    And on her dulcimer she played,
    Singing of Mount Abora.
    Could I revive within me
    Her symphony and song,
    To such a deep delight 'twould win me
That with music loud and long,
I would build that dome in air,
That sunny dome! those caves of ice!
And all who heard should see them there,
And all should cry, Beware! Beware!

His flashing eyes, his floating hair!
Weave a circle round him thrice,
And close your eyes with holy dread,
For he on honey-dew hath fed,
And drunk the milk of Paradise.
Samuel Taylor Coleridge.

Lycidas

YET once more, O ye laurels, and once more,
Ye myrtles brown, with ivy never sere,
I come, to pluck your berries harsh and crude,
And with forced fingers rude
Shatter your leaves before the mellowing year.
Bitter constraint and sad occasion dear
Compels me to disturb your season due:
For Lycidas is dead, dead ere his prime,
Young Lycidas, and hath not left his peer:
Who would not sing for Lycidas? He knew,
Himself to sing, and build the lofty rhyme.
He must not float upon his watery bier
Unwept, and welter to the parching wind
Without the meed of some melodious tear.

  Begin, then, sisters of the sacred well
That from beneath the seat of Jove doth spring;
Begin, and somewhat loudly sweep the string;
Hence with denial vain, and coy excuse:

So may some gentle muse
With lucky words favour my destined urn,
And, as he passes, turn,
And bid fair peace be to my sable shroud.

  For we were nursed upon the self-same hill,
Fed the same flock, by fountain, shade, and rill.
Together both, ere the high lawns appeared
Under the opening eyelids of the morn,
We drove a-field, and both together heard
What time the gray-fly winds her sultry horn,
Battening our flocks with the fresh dews of night,
Oft till the star that rose at evening bright
Toward heaven's descent had sloped his westering wheel.
Meanwhile the rural ditties were not mute,
Tempered to the oaten flute;
Rough satyrs danced, and fauns with cloven heel
From the glad sound would not be absent long:
And old Damœtas loved to hear our song.

  But, oh! the heavy change, now thou art gone,
Now thou art gone and never must return!
Thee, Shepherd, thee the woods, and desert caves,
With wild thyme and the gadding vine o'ergrown,

And all their echoes, mourn:
The willows, and the hazel copses green,
Shall now no more be seen
Fanning their joyous leaves to thy soft lays.
As killing as the canker to the rose,
Or taint-worm to the weanling herds that graze,
Or frost to flowers that their gay wardrobe wear
When first the white-thorn blows;
Such, Lycidas, thy loss to shepherd's ear.
 Where were ye, Nymphs, when the remorseless deep
Closed o'er the head of your loved Lycidas?
For neither were ye playing on the steep
Where your old bards, the famous Druids, lie,
Nor on the shaggy top of Mona high,
Nor yet where Deva spreads her wizard stream:
Ah me! I fondly dream,
Had ye been there: for what could that have done?
What could the Muse herself that Orpheus bore
The Muse herself, for her enchanting son
Whom universal nature did lament,
When by the rout that made the hideous roar
His gory visage down the stream was sent,
Down the swift Hebrus to the Lesbian shore?

Alas! what boots it with incessant care
To tend the homely, slighted, shepherd's trade,
And strictly meditate the thankless Muse?
Were it not better done, as others use,
To sport with Amaryllis in the shade,
Or with the tangles of Neæra's hair?
Fame is the spur that the clear spirit doth raise
(That last infirmity of noble minds)
To scorn delights and live laborious days:
But the fair guerdon when we hope to find,
And think to burst out into sudden blaze,
Comes the blind Fury with the abhorred shears
And slits the thin-spun life. "But not the praise,"
Phœbus replied, and touched my trembling ears;
"Fame is no plant that grows on mortal soil,
Nor in the glistening foil
Set off to the world, nor in broad rumour lies,
But lives and spreads aloft by those pure eyes
And perfect witness of all-judging Jove:
As he pronounces lastly on each deed,
Of so much fame in heaven except thy meed."—
  O fountain Arethuse, and thou honoured flood,
Smooth-sliding Mincius, crowned with vocal reeds,

That strain I heard was of a higher mood:
But now my oat proceeds,
And listens to the herald of the sea
That came in Neptune's plea;
He asked the waves, and asked the felon winds,
What hard mishap hath doomed this gentle swain?
And questioned every gust, of rugged winds,
That blows from off each beakéd promontory:
They knew not of his story;
And sage Hippotades their answer brings,
That not a blast was from his dungeon strayed,
The air was calm, and on the level brine
Sleek Panope with all her sisters played,
It was that fatal and perfidious bark,
Built in the eclipse, and rigged with curses dark,
That sunk so low that sacred head of thine.
  Next, Camus, reverend sire, went footing slow,
His mantle hairy, and his bonnet sedge
Inwrought with figures dim and on the edge
Like to that sanguine flower inscribed with woe.
"Ah! who hath reft," quoth he, "my dearest pledge!"—
Last came, and last did go,
The pilot of the Galilean lake.

Two massy keys he bore, of metals twain,
The golden opes, the iron shuts amain,
He shook his mitred locks, and stern bespake;
"How well could I have spared for thee, young swain,
Enow of such as, for their bellies' sake,
Creep, and intrude, and climb into the fold!
Of other care they little reckoning make
Than how to scramble at the shearers' feast
And shove away the worthy bidden guest;
Blind mouths! that scarce themselves know how to hold
A sheep-hook, or have learned aught else the least
That to the faithful herdsman's art belongs!
What recks it them? What need they? They are sped,
And, when they list, their lean and flashy songs
Grate on their scrannel pipes of wretched straw:
The hungry sheep look up, and are not fed,
But, swoln with wind and the rank mist they draw,
Rot inwardly, and foul contagion spread;
Besides what the grim wolf, with privy paw,
Daily devours apace, and nothing said:
But that two-handed engine at the door
Stands ready to smite once, and smite no more."—

Return, Alpheus, the dread voice is past,
That shrunk thy streams; return, Sicilian Muse,
And call the vales, and bid them hither cast
Their bells and flowerets of a thousand hues.
Ye valleys low, where the mild whispers use
Of shades, and wanton winds, and gushing brooks,
On whose fresh lap the swart star sparely looks,
Throw hither all your quaint enamelled eyes
That on the green turf suck the honeyed showers,
And purple all the ground with vernal flowers.
Bring the rathe primrose that forsaken dies,
The tufted crow-toe, and pale jessamine,
The white pink, and the pansy freaked with jet,
The glowing violet,
The musk-rose, and the well-attired woodbine,
With cowslips wan that hang the pensive head,
And every flower that sad embroidery wears;
Bid amaranthus all his beauty shed,
And daffodillies fill their cups with tears,
To strew the laureate hearse where Lycid lies.
For so, to interpose a little ease,
Let our frail thoughts dally with false surmise:
Ah me! whilst thee the shores and sounding seas

Wash far away, where'er thy bones are hurled,
Whether beyond the stormy Hebrides,
Where thou, perhaps under the whelming tide,
Visit'st the bottom of the monstrous world;
Or whether thou, to our moist vows denied,
Sleep'st by the fable of Bellerus old,
Where the great vision of the guarded mount
Looks toward Namancos and Bayona's hold:
Look homeward, angel, now, and melt with ruth;
And, O ye dolphins, waft the hapless youth.

  Weep no more, woeful shepherds, weep no more
For Lycidas, your sorrow, is not dead,
Sunk though he be beneath the watery floor.
So sinks the day-star in the ocean-bed,
And yet anon repairs his drooping head,
And tricks his beams, and, with new spangled ore,
Flames in the forehead of the morning sky:
So Lycidas sunk low, but mounted high,
Through the dear might of Him that walked the waves,
Where, other groves and other streams along,
With nectar pure his oozy locks he laves,
And hears the unexpressive nuptial song
In the blest kingdoms meek of joy and love,
There entertain him all the saints above,
In solemn troops and sweet societies

That sing, and, singing, in their glory move,
And wipe the tears for ever from his eyes.
Now, Lycidas, the shepherds weep no more;
Henceforth thou art the genius of the shore
In thy large recompense, and shalt be good
To all that wander in that perilous flood.

    Thus sang the uncouth swain to the oaks and rills,
While the still morn went out with sandals gray;
He touched the tender stops of various quills,
With eager thought warbling his Doric lay:
And now the sun had stretched out all the hills,
And now was dropt into the western bay:
At last he rose, and twitched his mantle blue:
To-morrow to fresh woods and pastures new.

                  John Milton.

Ode on Intimations of Immortality from Recollections of Early Childhood

> The Child is father of the Man;
> And I could wish my days to be
> Bound each to each by natural piety.

I

THERE was a time when meadow, grove, and stream,
The earth, and every common sight,
    To me did seem

Apparelled in celestial light,
The glory and the freshness of a dream.
It is not now as it hath been of yore;—
    Turn wheresoe'er I may,
        By night or day,
The things which I have seen I now can see no more.

II

The Rainbow comes and goes,
    And lovely is the Rose;
    The Moon doth with delight
Look round her when the heavens are bare;
    Waters on a starry night
    Are beautiful and fair;
The sunshine is a glorious birth;
But yet I know, where'er I go,
That there hath passed away a glory from the earth.

III

Now, while the Birds thus sing a joyous song,
    And while the young Lambs bound
        As to the tabor's sound,
To me alone there came a thought of grief:
A timely utterance gave that thought relief,
    And I again am strong.
The Cataracts blow their trumpets from the steep;

No more shall grief of mine the season wrong;
I hear the Echoes through the mountains throng,
The Winds come to me from the fields of sleep,
    And all the earth is gay;
      Land and Sea
   Give themselves up to jollity,
    And with the heart of May
Doth every Beast keep holiday;—
     Thou Child of Joy,
Shout round me, let me hear thy shouts, thou happy Shepherd-boy!

IV

Ye blessèd Creatures, I have heard the call
   Ye to each other make; I see
The heavens laugh with you in your jubilee;
   My heart is at your festival,
    My head hath its coronal,
The fulness of your bliss, I feel—I feel it all.
   Oh evil day! if I were sullen
    While Earth herself is adorning
     This sweet May morning,
    And the Children are culling
     On every side,
   In a thousand valleys far and wide,
   Fresh flowers; while the sun shines warm,

And the Babe leaps up on his Mother's arm:—
    I hear, I hear, with joy I hear!
    —But there's a Tree, of many, one,
A single Field which I have looked upon,
Both of them speak of something that is gone:
      The Pansy at my feet
      Doth the same tale repeat:
Whither is fled the visionary gleam?
Where is it now, the glory and the dream?

v

Our birth is but a sleep and a forgetting:
The Soul that rises with us, our life's Star,
    Hath had elsewhere its setting,
    And cometh from afar:
    Not in entire forgetfulness,
    And not in utter nakedness,
But trailing clouds of glory do we come
    From God, who is our home:
Heaven lies about us in our infancy!
Shades of the prison-house begin to close
    Upon the growing Boy,
But he beholds the light, and whence it flows,
    He sees it in his joy;
The Youth, who daily farther from the East
    Must travel, still is Nature's Priest,
      And by the vision splendid
      Is on his way attended;

At length the Man perceives it die away,
And fade into the light of common day.

VI

Earth fills her lap with pleasures of her own;
Yearnings she hath in her own natural kind,
And even with something of a Mother's mind,
    And no unworthy aim,
  The homely Nurse doth all she can
To make her Foster-child, her Inmate Man,
    Forget the glories he hath known,
And that imperial palace whence he came.

VII

Behold the Child among his new-born blisses,
A six years' darling of a pigmy size!
See, where 'mid work of his own hand he lies,
Fretted by sallies of his Mother's kisses,
With light upon him from his Father's eyes!
See, at his feet, some little plan or chart,
Some fragment from his dream of human life,
Shaped by himself with newly-learned art;
    A wedding or a festival,
    A mourning or a funeral;
      And this hath now his heart,
    And unto this he frames his song:
      Then will he fit his tongue
To dialogues of business, love, or strife:

  But it will not be long
  Ere this be thrown aside,
  And with new joy and pride
The little Actor cons another part;
Filling from time to time his "humorous stage"
With all the Persons, down to palsied Age,
That Life brings with her in her equipage;
  As if his whole vocation
  Were endless imitation.

VIII

Thou, whose exterior semblance doth belie
  Thy Soul's immensity;
Thou best Philosopher, who yet dost keep
Thy heritage, thou Eye among the blind,
That, deaf and silent, read'st the eternal deep,
Haunted for ever by the eternal mind,—
  Mighty Prophet! Seer blest!
  On whom those truths do rest,
Which we are toiling all our lives to find,
In darkness lost, the darkness of the grave;
Thou, over whom thy Immortality
Broods like the Day, a master o'er a Slave,
A Presence which is not to be put by;
Thou little Child, yet glorious in the might
Of heaven-born freedom on thy being's height,
Why with such earnest pains dost thou provoke

The years to bring the inevitable yoke,
Thus blindly with thy blessedness at strife?
Full soon thy Soul shall have her earthly
    freight,
And custom lie upon thee with a weight,
Heavy as frost, and deep almost as life!

IX

    O joy! that in our embers
    Is something that doth live,
    That nature yet remembers
    What was so fugitive!
The thought of our past years in me doth
    breed
Perpetual benediction: not indeed
For that which is most worthy to be blest;
Delight and liberty, the simple creed
Of Childhood, whether busy or at rest,
With new-fledged hope still fluttering in his
    breast:—
    Not for these I raise
    The song of thanks and praise;
  But for those obstinate questionings
  Of sense and outward things,
  Fallings from us, vanishings;
  Blank misgivings of a Creature
Moving about in worlds not realised,
High instincts before which our mortal Nature
Did tremble like a guilty thing surprised:

But for those first affections,
Those shadowy recollections,
   Which, be they what they may,
Are yet the fountain light of all our day,
Are yet a master light of all our seeing;
   Uphold us, cherish, and have power to make
Our noisy years seem moments in the being
Of the eternal Silence: truths that wake,
      To perish never;
Which neither listlessness, nor mad endeavour
      Nor Man nor Boy,
Nor all that is at enmity with joy,
Can utterly abolish or destroy!
   Hence, in a season of calm weather,
      Though inland far we be,
Our Souls have sight of that immortal sea
      Which brought us hither,
      Can in a moment travel thither
And see the children sport upon the shore,
And hear the mighty waters rolling evermore.

x

Then sing, ye Birds, sing, sing a joyous song!
   And let the young Lambs bound
   As to the tabor's sound!
We in thought will join your throng
   Ye that pipe and ye that play,
   Ye that through your hearts to-day

  Feel the gladness of the May!
What though the radiance which was once so bright
Be now for ever taken from my sight,
  Though nothing can bring back the hour
Of splendour in the grass, of glory in the flower;
   We will grieve not, rather find
   Strength in what remains behind;
   In the primal sympathy
   Which having been must ever be;
   In the soothing thoughts that spring
   Out of human suffering;
   In the faith that looks through death,
In years that bring the philosophic mind.

XI

And O, ye Fountains, Meadows, Hills, and Groves,
Forebode not any severing of our loves!
Yet in my heart of hearts I feel your might;
I only have relinquished one delight
To live beneath your more habitual sway.
I love the Brooks, which down their channels fret,
Even more than when I tripped lightly as they:
The innocent brightness of a new-born Day
  Is lovely yet;

The Clouds that gather round the setting sun
Do take a sober colouring from an eye
That hath kept watch o'er man's mortality;
Another race hath been, and other palms are
   won.
Thanks to the human heart by which we live,
Thanks to its tenderness, its joys, its fears,
To me the meanest flower that blows can give
Thoughts that do often lie too deep for tears.
            William Wordsworth.

THE SEA AND THE RIVER

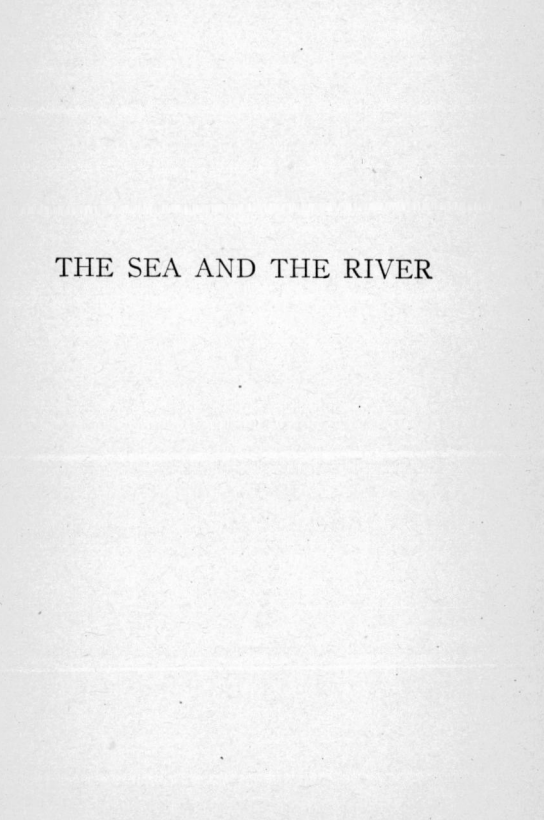

I will go back to the great sweet mother,
    Mother and lover of men, the sea.
I will go down to her, I and none other,
    Close with her, kiss her and mix her with me;
Cling to her, strive with her, hold her fast;
O fair white mother, in days long past
Born without sister, born without brother,
    Set free my soul as thy soul is free.
                Algernon Charles Swinburne.

As the stars come out, and the night-wind
Brings up the stream
Murmurs and scents of the infinite sea.
                Matthew Arnold.

O to sail in a ship,
To leave this steady unendurable land,
To leave the tiresome sameness of the streets, the sidewalks and the houses,
To leave you, O you solid motionless land, and entering a ship,
To sail and sail and sail!
                Walt Whitman.

Salt and Sunny Days

(From *To Cicely N. Marston*)

OH, silent glory of the summer day!
  How, then, we watched with glad and
    indolent eyes
The white-sailed ships dream on their shining
    way,
  Till, fading, they were mingled with the
    skies.
Have we not watched her, too, on nights that
    steep
  The soul in peace of moonlight, softly move
As a most passionate maiden, who in sleep
  Laughs low, and tosses in a dream of love?

And when the heat broke up, and in its place,
  Came the strong, shouting days and nights,
    that run,
All white with stars, across the labouring
    ways
  Of billows warm with storm, instead of sun,

In gray and desolate twilights, when no feet
   Save ours might dare the shore, did we not come
Through winds that all in vain against us beat
   Until we had the warm sweet-smelling foam
Full in our faces, and the frantic wind
   Shrieked round us, and our cheeks grew numb, then warm,
Until we felt our souls, no more confined,
   Mix with the waves, and strain against the storm?
Oh! the immense, illimitable delight
   It is, to stand by some tempestuous bay,
What time the great sea waxes warm and white
   And beats and blinds the following wind with spray!

Philip Bourke Marston.

The Sea Gypsy

I AM fevered with the sunset,
   I am fretful with the bay,
For the wander-thirst is on me
   And my soul is in Cathay.

There's a schooner in the offing,
   With her topsails shot with fire,
And my heart has gone aboard her
   For the Islands of Desire.

I must forth again to-morrow!
With the sunset I must be
Hull down on the trail of rapture
In the wonder of the Sea.
Richard Hovey.

Sailor's Song

TO sea, to sea! The calm is o'er;
   The wanton water leaps in sport,
And rattles down the pebbly shore;
   The dolphin wheels, the sea-cows snort,
And unseen mermaids' pearly song
Comes bubbling up, the weeds among.
   Fling broad the sail, dip deep the oar:
   To sea, to sea! the calm is o'er.

To sea, to sea! our wide-winged bark
   Shall billowy cleave its sunny way,
And with its shadow, fleet and dark,
   Break the caved Tritons' azure day,
Like mighty eagle soaring light
O'er antelopes on Alpine height.
   The anchor heaves, the ship swings free,
   The sails swell full. To sea, to sea!
Thomas Lovell Beddoes.

The Wander-Lovers

Down the world with Marna!
  That's the life for me!
Wandering with the wandering wind,
Vagabond and unconfined!
Roving with the roving rain
Its unboundaried domain!
Kith and kin of wander-kind
Children of the sea!

Petrels of the sea-drift!
Swallows of the lea!
Arabs of the whole wide girth
Of the wind-encircled earth!
In all climes we pitch our tents,
Cronies of the elements
With the secret lords of birth
Intimate and free.

All the seaboard knows us
From Fundy to the Keys;
Every bend and every creek
Of abundant Chesapeake;
Ardise hills and Newport coves
And the far-off orange groves
Where Floridian oceans break,
Tropic tiger seas.

Down the world with Marna,
Tarrying there and here!
Just as much at home in Spain
As in Tangier or Touraine!
Shakespeare's Avon knows us well,
And the crags of Neufchâtel;
And the ancient Nile is fain
Of our coming near.

Down the world with Marna,
Daughter of the air!
Marna of the subtle grace,
And the vision in her face!
Moving in the measures trod
By the angels before God!
With her sky-blue eyes amaze
And her sea-blue hair!

Marna with the trees' life
In her veins a-stir!
Marna of the aspen heart
Where the sudden quivers start!
Quick-responsive, subtle, wild!
Artless as an artless child,
Spite of all her reach of art!
Oh, to roam with her!

Marna with the wind's will,
Daughter of the sea!
Marna of the quick disdain,
Starting at the dream of stain!

At a smile with love aglow,
At a frown a statued woe,
Standing pinnacled in pain
Till a kiss sets free!

Down the world with Marna,
Daughter of the fire!
Marna of the deathless hope
Still alert to win new scope
Where the wings of life may spread
For a flight unhazarded!
Dreamy of the speech to cope
With the heart's desire.

Marna of the far quest
After the divine!
Striving ever for some goal
Past the blunder-god's control!
Dreaming of potential years
When no day shall dawn in fears!
That's the Marna of my soul,
Wander-bride of mine!

Richard Hovey.

The River and the Sea
(From *Will o' the Mill*)

ONE evening he asked the miller where the river went.

"It goes down the valley," answered he, "and turns a power of mills—six score mills, they say, from here to Unterdeck—and it none the wearier after all. And then it goes out into the lowlands, and waters the great corn country, and runs through a sight of fine cities (so they say) where kings live all alone in great palaces, with a sentry walking up and down before the door. And it goes under bridges with stone men upon them, looking down and smiling so curious at the water, and living folks leaning their elbows on the wall and looking over too. And then it goes on and on, and down through marshes and sands, until at last it falls into the sea, where the ships are that bring parrots and tobacco from the Indies. Ay, it has a long trot before it as it goes singing over our weir, bless its heart!"

"And what is the sea?" asked Will.

"The sea!" cried the miller. "Lord help us all, it is the greatest thing God made! That is where all the water in the world runs down into a great salt lake. There it lies, as flat as my hand and as innocent-like as a child; but they do say when the wind blows it gets up into water-mountains bigger than any of ours, and swallows down great ships bigger than our mill, and makes such a roaring that you can hear it miles away upon the land. There are great fish in it five times bigger than a bull, and one old serpent as long as our river and as old as all the world, with whiskers like a man, and a crown of silver on her head."

R. L. Stevenson.

The Brook

I COME from haunts of coot and hern,
   I make a sudden sally,
And sparkle out among the fern,
   To bicker down a valley.

By thirty hills I hurry down,
   Or slip between the ridges,
By twenty thorps, a little town,
   And half a hundred bridges.

Till last by Philip's farm I flow
   To join the brimming river,
For men may come and men may go,
   But I go on for ever.

I chatter over stony ways,
   In little sharps and trebles,
I bubble into eddying bays,
   I babble on the pebbles.

With many a curve my banks I fret
   By many a field and fallow,
And many a fairy foreland set
   With willow-weed and mallow.

I chatter, chatter, as I flow
   To join the brimming river,
For men may come and men may go,
   But I go on for ever.

I wind about, and in and out,
   With here a blossom sailing,
And here and there a lusty trout,
   And here and there a grayling,

And here and there a foamy flake
   Upon me, as I travel
With many a silvery waterbreak
   Above the golden gravel,

And draw them all along, and flow
   To join the brimming river,
For men may come and men may go,
   But I go on for ever.

I steal by lawns and grassy plots,
   I slide by hazel covers;
I move the sweet forget-me-nots
   That grow for happy lovers.

I slip, I slide, I gloom, I glance,
   Among my skimming swallows;
I make the netted sunbeam dance
   Against my sandy shallows.

I murmur under moon and stars
　　In brambly wildernesses;
I linger by my shingly bars;
　　I loiter round my cresses;

And out again I curve and flow
　　To join the brimming river,
For men may come and men may go,
　　But I go on for ever.
　　　　　　　　Alfred, Lord Tennyson.

At Sea

BUT the mere fact of its being a tramp ship gave us many comforts; we could cut about with the men and officers, stay in the wheel-house, discuss all manner of things, and really be a little at sea. And truly there is nothing else. I had literally forgotten what happiness was, and the full mind—full of external and physical things, not full of cares and labours and rot about a fellow's behaviour. My heart literally sang: I truly care for nothing so much as that.

From one of R. L. Stevenson's Letters.

THE REDDENING LEAF

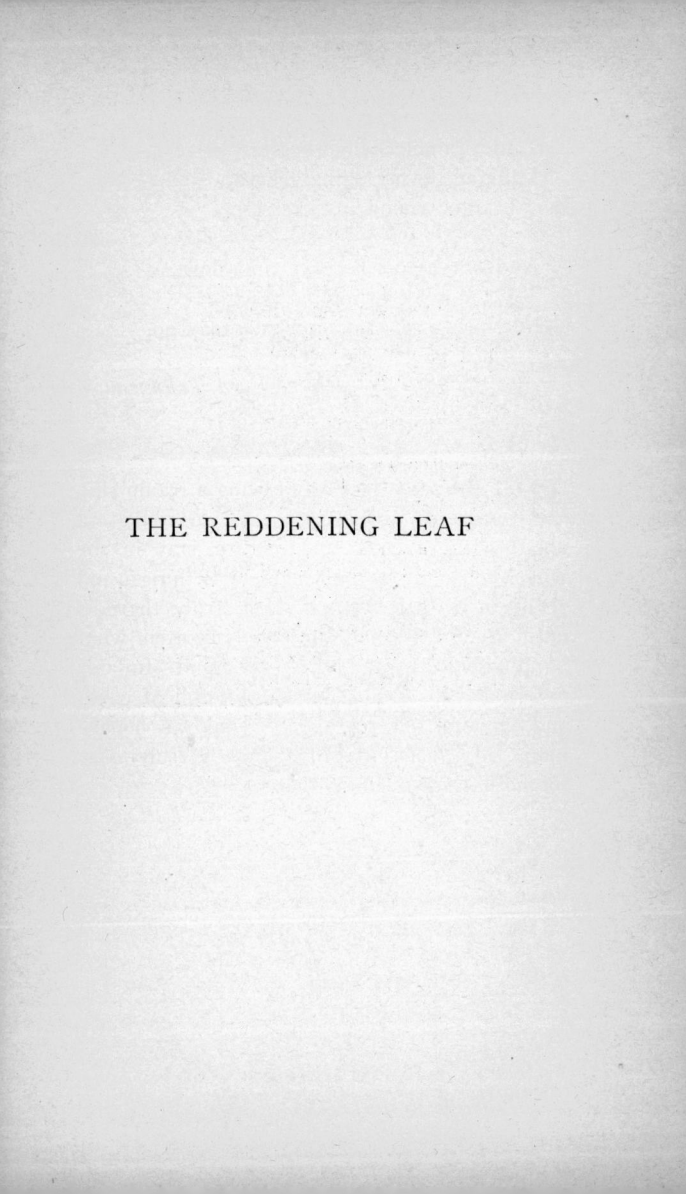

Laden deep with fruity cluster,
  Then September, ripe and hale;
Bees about his basket fluster,—
Laden deep with fruity cluster.
Skies have now a softer lustre;
  Barns resound to flap of flail.

Thou then, too, of woodlands lover,
  Dusk October, berry-stained;
Wailed about of parting plover,—
Thou then, too, of woodlands lover.
Fading now are copse and cover;
  Forests now are sere and waned.
                              Austin Dobson.

Lo! sweeten'd with the summer light,
The full juiced apple, waxing over-mellow,
Drops in a silent autumn night.
               Alfred, Lord Tennyson.

To Autumn   ～ ～ ～ ～

SEASON of mists and mellow fruitfulness,
    Close bosom-friend of the maturing sun;
Conspiring with him how to load and bless
    With fruit the vines that round the thatch-eaves run;
To bend with apples the moss'd cottage-trees,
    And fill all fruit with ripeness to the core;
        To swell the gourd, and plump the hazel shells
With a sweet kernel; to set budding more,
    And still more, later flowers for the bees,
    Until they think warm days will never cease,
        For Summer has o'er-brimm'd their clammy cells.

Who hath not seen thee oft amid thy store?
    Sometimes whoever seeks abroad may find
Thee sitting careless on a granary floor,
    Thy hair soft-lifted by the winnowing wind;
Or on a half-reap'd furrow sound asleep,

Drows'd with the fume of poppies, while thy hook
Spares the next swath and all its twined flowers:
And sometimes like a gleaner thou dost keep
Steady thy laden head across a brook;
Or by a cyder-press, with patient look,
Thou watchest the last oozings hours by hours.

Where are the songs of Spring? Ay, where are they?
Think not of them, thou hast thy music too,—
While barred clouds bloom the soft-dying day,
And touch the stubble-plains with rosy hue;
Then in a wailful choir the small gnats mourn
Among the river sallows, borne aloft
Or sinking as the light wind lives or dies;
And full-grown lambs loud bleat from hilly bourn;
Hedge-crickets sing; and now with treble soft
The red-breast whistles from a garden-croft;
And gathering swallows twitter in the skies.

John Keats.

Sweet Fern

THE subtle power in perfume found
  Nor priest nor sibyl vainly learned;
On Grecian shrine or Aztec mound
  No censer idly burned.

That power the old-time worships knew,
  The Corybantes' frenzied dance,
The Pythian priestess swooning through
  The wonderland of trance.

And Nature holds, in wood and field,
  Her thousand sunlit censers still;
To spells of flower and shrub we yield
  Against or with our will.

I climbed a hill path strange and new
  With slow feet, pausing at each turn;
A sudden waft of west wind blew
  The breath of the sweet fern.

That fragrance from my vision swept
  The alien landscape; in its stead,
Up fairer hills of youth I stepped,
  As light of heart as tread.

I saw my boyhood's lakelet shine
  Once more through rifts of woodland shade;
I knew my river's winding line
  By morning mist betrayed.

With me June's freshness, lapsing brook,
   Murmurs of leaf and bee, the call
Of birds, and one in voice and look
   In keeping with them all.

A fern beside the way we went
   She plucked, and smiling, held it up,
While from her hand the wild, sweet scent
   I drank as from a cup.

O potent witchery of smell!
   The dust-dry leaves to life return,
And she who plucked them owns the spell
   And lifts her ghostly fern.

Or sense or spirit? Who shall say
   What touch the chord of memory thrills?
It passed, and left the August day
   Ablaze on lonely hills.
John Greenleaf Whittier.

Autumn

THE year grows still again, the surging wake
   Of full-sailed summer folds its furrows up,
     As after passing of an argosy
     Old Silence settles back upon the sea,
   And ocean grows as placid as a cup.
     Spring, the young morn, and Summer, the strong noon,

Have dreamed and done and died for Autumn's sake:
Autumn that finds not for a loss so dear
  Solace in stack and garner hers too soon—soon—
  Autumn, the faithful widow of the year.
Autumn, a poet once so full of song,
  Wise in all rhymes of blossom and of bud,
Hath lost the early magic of his tongue,
  And hath no passion in his failing blood.
Hear ye no sound of sobbing in the air?
  'Tis his. Low bending in a secret lane,
Late blooms of second childhood in his hair,
  He tries old magic, like a dotard mage;
  Tries spell and spell, to weep and try again:
Yet not a daisy hears, and everywhere
  The hedgrow rattles like an empty cage.
He hath no pleasure in his silken skies,
  Nor delicate ardours of the yellow land;
Yea, dead, for all its gold, the woodland lies,
  And all the throats of music filled with sand.
  Neither to him across the stubble field
May stack nor garner any comfort bring,
  Who loveth more this jasmine he hath made,
  The little tender rhyme he yet can sing,
Than yesterday, with all its pompous yield,
  Or all its shaken laurels on his head.

Richard Le Gallienne.

Carn A-Turnen Yoller

THE copse ha' got his shiady boughs,
    Wi' blackbirds' evemen whissles;
The hills ha' sheep upon ther brows,
    The zummerleäze ha' thissles.
The meäds be gay in grassy May,
    But O vrom hill to holler,
Let I look down upon a groun'
    O' carn a-turnen yoller.

An' pease da grow in tangled beds,
    An' beäns be sweet to snuff, O;
The tiaper woats da bend ther heads
    The barley's beard is rough, O;
The turnip green is fresh between
    The carn in hill ar holler,
But I'd look down upon the groun'
    O' wheat a-turnen yoller.

'Tis merry when the brawny men
    Da come to reap it down, O,
Wher glossy red the poppy head
    'S among the sta'ks so brown, O;
'Tis merry while the wheat's in hile
    Ar when, by hill ar holler,
The leäzers thick da stoop to pick
    The ears so ripe an' yoller.

William Barnes.

On Wenlock Edge

ON Wenlock Edge the wood's in trouble;
   His forest fleece the Wrekin heaves;
The gale, it plies the saplings double,
And thick on Severn snow the leaves.

'Twould blow like this through holt and hanger
Where Uricon the city stood:
'Tis the old wind in the old anger,
But then it threshed another wood.

Then, 'twas before my time, the Roman
At yonder heaving hill would stare;
The blood that warms an English yeoman,
The thoughts that hurt him, they were there.

There, like the wind through woods in riot,
Through him the gale of life blew high;
The tree of man was never quiet:
Then 'twas the Roman, now 'tis I.

The gale, it plies the saplings double,
It blows so hard, 'twill soon be gone:
To-day the Roman and his trouble
Are ashes under Uricon.

A. E. Housman.

The Joys of Fowling

OF all the joys that sporting yields,
　　Give me to beat the stubble-fields
Quite early in September:
A brace of pointers, staunch and true,
A gun that kills whate'er I view,
I care not whether old or new,
　　Are things one must remember.

Old Ponto makes a famous point,
As marble stiff, in ev'ry joint.
　　I cautiously proceed,
When quickly up the covey fly—
Bang, bang—both barrels then I try—
And lo! a brace before me die,
　　The shooter's richest meed.

If hares I want for friends in town,
I can tell where to knock them down
　　Within the furze-bush cover.
A leash I bag, then homeward go,
My spirits all in joyous flow,
And more delight, I'm sure, I know,
　　Than doth a beauty's lover.

In wintry woods, when leaves are dead,
And hedges beam with berries red,
　　The pheasant is my spoil.
Fenc'd with high gaiters out I go,
And beat through tangled bushes low;

Each joy of mine my spaniels know,
  Though wand'ring many a mile.

At night return'd, my bag well fill'd,
Perchance four brace of pheasants kill'd,
  I sit me down in peace,
And envy not ambition's cares,
Nor e'en the crown a monarch wears,
Such joys as mine he seldom shares—
  Oh, may that joy ne'er cease.
              Old Song.

The Music of the Pack

IF you would have your kennel for sweetness of cry, then you must compound it of some large dogs, that have deep solemn Mouthes, and are swift in spending, which must as it were bear the base in the consort; then a double number of roaring and loud ringing Mouthes, which must bear the counter tenor; then some hollow plain sweet Mouthes, which must bear the mean or middle part; and so with these three parts of musick you shall make your cry perfect: and herein you shall observe that these Hounds thus mixt, do run just and even together and not hang off loose from one another, which is the vilest sight that may be; and you shall understand, that this composition is best to be made of the swiftest and largest deep mouthed dog, the slowest middle siz'd dog, and the shortest legg'd slender dog. Amongst these you may cast in a couple or two small single beagles, which as small trebles may warble amongst them: the cry will be a great deal the more sweet. . . . If you would have your kennel for depth of mouth, then you shall compound it of the largest dogs which have the greatest mouths and deepest slews, such as your West Country, Che-shire and Lancashire dogs are, and to five or six base couple of mouths shall not add above two couple of counter tenors, as many means, and not above one couple of Roarers, which being heard but now and then, as at the opening or hitting of a scent, will give much sweetness to the solemnness and graveness of the cry, and the musick thereof will be much more delightfull to the ears of every beholder.

Gervase Markham.

NIGHT AND THE STARS

Hail, Twilight, sovereign of one peaceful hour!
Not dull art Thou as undiscerning Night;
But studious only to remove from sight
Day's mutable distinctions. Ancient Power!
Thus did the waters gleam, the mountains lower
To the rude Briton, when, in wolf-skin vest
Here roving wild, he laid him down to rest
On the bare rock, or through a leafy bower
Look'd ere his eyes were closed. By him was seen
The self same vision which we now behold,
At thy meek bidding, shadowy Power, brought forth:
These mighty barriers, and the gulf between;
The flood, the stars;—a spectacle as old
As the beginning of the heavens and earth!
William Wordsworth.

To the Evening Star

THOU fair-haired Angel of the Evening,
    Now whilst the sun rests on the mountains, light
Thy bright torch of love; thy radiant crown
Put on, and smile upon our evening bed!
Smile on our loves; and while thou drawest the
Blue curtains of the sky, scatter thy silver dew
On every flower that shuts its sweet eyes
In timely sleep. Let thy West Wind sleep on
The lake; speak silence with thy glimmering eyes
And wash the dusk with silver.—Soon, full soon,
Dost thou withdraw; then the wolf rages wide,
And the lion glares through the dun forest,
The fleeces of our flocks are covered with
Thy sacred dew; protect them with thine influence!

William Blake.

Evemen in the Village

NOW the light o' the west is a-turn'd to gloom;
An' the men be at huome vrom ground;
An' the bells be a-zenden al down the Coombe
A muoanen an' dyen sound.
An' the wind is still,
An' the house-dogs da bark,
An' the rooks be a-vled to the elems high an' dark,
An' the water da roar at mill.

An' out droo yander cottage's winder-piane
The light o' the candle da shoot,
An' young Jemmy the blacksmith is down the liane
A-playen his jarman-flute.
An' the miller's man
Da zit down at his ease
'Pon the girt wooden seat that is under the trees,
Wi' his pipe an' his cider can.

Tha' da za that 'tis zom'hat in towns to zee
Fresh fiazen vrom day to day:
Tha' mid zee em var me, ef the two or dree
I da love should but smile an' stay.

Zoo gi'e me the sky,
An' the air an' the zun,
An' a huome in the dell wher the water da run,
An' there let me live an' die.
William Barnes.

Night   ◇   ◇   ◇   ◇

THE sun descending in the west,
The evening star does shine;
The birds are silent in their nest,
And I must seek for mine.
The moon, like a flower
In heaven's high bower,
With silent delight
Sits and smiles on the night.

Farewell, green fields and happy grove,
Where flocks have ta'en delight;
Where lambs have nibbled, silent move
The feet of angels bright:
Unseen they pour blessing,
And joy without ceasing,
On each bud and blossom,
On each sleeping bosom.

They look in every thoughtless nest,
Where birds are covered warm;
They visit caves of every beast,
To keep them all from harm.

If they see any weeping
That should have been sleeping,
They pour sleep on their head,
And sit down by their bed.

When wolves and tigers howl for prey
They pitying stand and weep,
Seeking to drive their thirst away,
And keep them from the sheep.
But if they rush dreadful
The angels most heedful
Receive each mild spirit
New worlds to inherit.

And there the lion's ruddy eyes
Shall flow with tears of gold:
And pitying the tender cries,
And walking round the fold,
Saying: Wrath by His meekness,
And by His health sickness,
Are driven away
From our immortal day.

And now beside thee, bleating lamb,
I can lie down and sleep,
Or think on Him who bore thy name,
Graze after thee, and weep.
For, washed in life's river,
My bright mane for ever
Shall shine like the gold,
As I guard o'er the fold.   *William Blake.*

To Night

SWIFTLY walk o'er the western wave,
        Spirit of Night!
Out of the misty eastern cave
Where, all the long and lone daylight,
Thou wovest dreams of joy and fear
Which make thee terrible and dear,
        Swift be thy flight!

Wrap thy form in a mantle grey,
        Star-inwrought,
Blind with thine hair the eyes of Day;
Kiss her until she be wearied out.
Then wander o'er city, and sea, and land
Touching all with thine opiate wand—
        Come, long-sought!

When I arose and saw the dawn,
        I sighed for thee;
When light rode high, and the dew was gone,
And noon lay heavy on flower and tree,
And the weary Day turned to his rest,
Lingering like an unloved guest,
        I sighed for thee.

Thy brother Death came, and cried,
  "Would'st thou me?"
Thy sweet child Sleep, the filmy-eyed,
  Murmured like a noontide bee,

"Shall I nestle near thy side?
Would'st thou me?"—And I replied,
"No, not thee."

Death will come when thou art dead,
　　　Soon, too soon—
Sleep will come when thou art fled.
Of neither would I ask the boon
I ask of thee, belovèd Night—
Swift be thine approaching flight,
　　　Come soon, soon!
　　　　　　Percy Bysshe Shelley.

Orion

(From *Pagan Papers*)

THE moonless night has a touch of frost, and is steely-clear. High and dominant amidst the Populations of the Sky, the restless and the steadfast alike, hangs the great Plough, lit with a hard radiance as of the polished and shining share. And yonder, low on the horizon, but half resurgent as yet, crouches the magnificent Hunter: watchful, seemingly, and expectant: with some hint of menace in his port.

Yet should his game be up, you would think, by now. Many a century has passed since the plough first sped a conqueror east and west, clearing forest and draining fen; policing the valleys with barbed-wires and Sunday schools, with the chains that are forged of peace, the irking fetters of plenty: driving also the whole lot of us, these to sweat at its tail, those to plod with the patient team, but all to march in a great chain-gang, the convicts of peace and order and law: while the happy nomad, with his woodlands, his wild cattle, his pleasing nuptialities, has long since disappeared, dropping only in his flight some store of flintheads, a legacy of confusion. Truly, we Children of the Plough, but for yon tremendous Monitor in the sky, were in right case to forget that the Hunter is still a quantity to reckon withal. Where, then, does he hide the Shaker of the Spear? Why here, my brother, and here; deep in the breasts of each and all of us! And for this drop of primal quicksilver in the blood what poppy or mandragora shall purge it hence away?

Kenneth Grahame.

Sleep Beneath the Stars

(From *Travels with a Donkey in the Cevennes*)

NIGHT is a dead monotonous period under a roof; but in the open world it passes lightly, with its stars and dews and perfumes, and the hours are marked by changes in the face of Nature. What seems a kind of temporal death to people choked between walls and curtains, is only a light and living slumber to the man who sleeps a-field. All night long he can hear Nature breathing deeply and freely; even as she takes her rest, she turns and smiles; and there is one stirring hour unknown to those who dwell in houses, when a wakeful influence goes abroad over the sleeping hemisphere, and all the outdoor world are on their feet. It is then that the cock first crows, not this time to announce the dawn, but like a cheerful watchman speeding the course of night. Cattle awake on the meadows; sheep break their fast on dewy hillsides, and change to a new lair among the ferns; and houseless men, who have lain down with the fowls, open their dim eyes and behold the beauty of the night.

At what inaudible summons, at what gentle touch of Nature, are all these sleepers thus recalled in the same hour to life? Do the stars rain down an influence, or do we share some thrill of mother earth below our resting bodies? Even shepherds and old country-folk, who are the deepest read in these arcana, have not a guess as to the means or purpose of this nightly resurrection. Towards two in the morning they declare the thing takes place;

and neither know nor inquire further. And at least it is a pleasant incident. We are disturbed in our slumber only, like the luxurious *Montaigne,* "that we may the better and more sensibly relish it." We have a moment to look upon the stars. And there is a special pleasure for some minds in the reflection that we show the impulse with all out-door creatures in our neighbourhood, that we have escaped out of the *Bastille* of civilisation, and are become, for the time being a mere kindly animal and a sheep of Nature's flock.

R. L. Stevenson.

To Sleep ∾ ∾ ∾ ∾ ∾

A FLOCK of sheep that leisurely pass by,
   One after one; the sound of rain, and bees
Murmuring; the fall of rivers, winds, and seas,
Smooth fields, white sheets of water, and pure sky.
I've thought of all by turns; and yet do lie
Sleepless; and soon the small bird's melodies
Must hear first utter'd from my orchard trees,
And the first cuckoo's melancholy cry.
Even thus last night, and two nights more, I lay,

And could not win thee, Sleep! by any stealth:
So do not let me wear to-night away:
Without Thee what is all the morning's wealth?
Come, blessèd barrier between day and day,
Dear mother of fresh thoughts and joyous health!

William Wordsworth.

A LITTLE COMPANY OF GOOD
COUNTRY PEOPLE

With the open air and a leisurely life,
　　Homespun, and spaniels, and honey,
An eave-full of swallows, a sun-browned wife,
　　He's never a thought for money.
T. Farquharson

　　Simplify, simplify!
H. D. Thoreau.

The Barefoot Boy

BLESSINGS on thee, little man,
  Barefoot boy, with cheek of tan!
With thy turned-up pantaloons,
And thy merry whistled tunes;
With thy red lip, redder still
Kissed by strawberries on the hill;
With the sunshine on thy face,
Through thy torn brim's jaunty grace;
From my heart I give thee joy,—
I was once a barefoot boy.
  Prince thou art,—the grown-up man
Only is republican.
Let the million-dollared ride!
Barefoot, trudging at his side,
Thou hast more than he can buy
In the reach of ear and eye,—
Outward sunshine, inward joy:
Blessings on thee, barefoot boy!

Oh for boyhood's painless play,
Sleep that wakes in laughing day,
Health that mocks the doctor's rules,
Knowledge never learned of schools,
Of the wild bee's morning chase,

Of the wild flower's time and place,
Flight of fowl and habitude
Of the tenants of the wood;
How the tortoise bears his shell,
How the woodchuck digs his cell,
And the ground-mole sinks his well;
How the robin feeds her young,
How the oriole's nest is hung;
Where the whitest lilies blow,
Where the freshest berries grow,
Where the ground-nut trails its vine,
Where the wood-grape's clusters shine;
Of the black wasp's cunning way,
Mason of his walls of clay,
And the architectural plans
Of gray hornet artisans!
For, eschewing books and tasks,
Nature answers all he asks;
Hand in hand with her he walks,
Face to face with her he talks,
Part and parcel of her joy.—
Blessings on the barefoot boy!

Oh for boyhood's time of June,
Crowding years in one brief moon,
When all things I heard or saw,
Me, their master, waited for.
I was rich in flowers and trees,
Humming-birds and honey-bees;

For my sport the squirrel played,
Plied the snouted mole his spade;
For my taste the blackberry cone
Purpled over hedge and stone;
Laughed the brook for my delight
Through the day and through the night,
Whispering at the garden wall,
Talked with me from fall to fall;
Mine the sand-rimmed pickerel pond,
Mine the walnut slopes beyond,
Mine, on bending orchard trees,
Apples of Hesperides!
Still as my horizon grew,
Larger grew my riches too;
All the world I saw or knew
Seemed a complex Chinese toy,
Fashioned for a barefoot boy.

Oh for festal dainties spread,
Like my bowl of milk and bread;
Pewter spoon and bowl of wood,
On the door-stone, gray and rude!
O'er me, like a regal tent,
Cloudy ribbed, the sunset bent,
Purple-curtained, fringed with gold,
Looped in many a wind-swung fold;
While for music came the play
Of the pied frogs' orchestra;
And, to light the noisy choir,

Lit the fly his lamp of fire.
I was monarch: pomp and joy
Waited on the barefoot boy!

Cheerily, then, my little man,
Live and laugh, as boyhood can!
Though the flinty slopes be hard,
Stubble-speared the new-mown sward,
Every morn shall lead thee through
Fresh baptisms of the dew;
Every evening from thy feet
Shall the cool wind kiss the heat:
All too soon these feet must hide
In the prison cells of pride,
Lose the freedom of the sod,
Like a colt's for work be shod,
Made to tread the mills of toil,
Up and down in ceaseless moil:
Happy if their track be found
Never on forbidden ground;
Happy if they sink not in
Quick and treacherous sands of sin.
Ah! that thou couldst know thy joy,
Ere it passes, barefoot boy!

John Greenleaf Whittier.

The Milkmaid

WHAT a dainty life the milkmaid leads,
　　When over the flowery meads

She dabbles in the dew
And sings to her cow,
And feels not the pain
Of love or disdain!
She sleeps in the night, though she toils in the
    day,
And merrily passeth her time away.
Thomas Nabbes.

The Shepherd o' the Farm

I BE the Shepherd o' the farm;
    An' be so proud a-roven round
Wi' my long crook a-thirt my yarm,
    As ef I wer a king a-crown'd.

An' I da bide al day among
    The bleäten sheep, an' pitch ther vuold;
An' when the evemen shiades be long
    Da zee 'em al a-penn'd an' tuold.

An' I da zee the frisken lam's,
    Wi' swingen tails and woolly lags,
A-playen roun' ther veeden dams,
    An' pullen o' ther milky bags.

An' I, bezide a hawtharn tree,
    Da zit upon the zunny down,
While shiades o' zummer clouds da vlee
    Wi' silent flight along the groun'.

An' there, among the many cries
   O' sheep an' lam's, my dog da pass
A zultry hour wi' blinken eyes,
   An' nose a-stratch'd upon the grass.

But in a twinklen, at my word,
   The shaggy rogue is up an' gone
Out roun' the sheep lik' any bird,
   To do what he's a-zent upon.

An' wi' my zong, an' wi' my fife,
   An' wi' my hut o' turf an' hurdles,
I wou'den channge my shepherd's life
   To be a-miade a king o' wordles.

An' I da goo to washen pool,
   A-sousen auver head an' ears
The shaggy sheep, to cleän ther wool,
   An' miake 'em ready var the shears.

An' when the shearen time da come,
   I be at barn vrom dawn till dark,
Wher zome da catch the sheep, and zome
   Da mark ther zides wi' miaster's mark.

An' when the shearen's al a-done,
   Then we da eat, an' drink, an' zing
In miaster's kitchen, till the tun
   Wi' merry sounds do shiake an' ring.

I be the Shepherd o' the farm:
   An' be so proud a-roven round
Wi' my long crook a-thirt my yarm,
   As ef I were a king a-crown'd.
William Barnes.

The Shepherd

(From *Pan and the Young Shepherd*)

YOUR shepherd is very near to Earth. He grows up from her lap, he never quite leaves her bosom; he is her foster-child. He may hear her heart-beats and drink of her tears. If she smiles he knoweth why. He has listened and he knoweth. She telleth him her secret thoughts; all the day long he may lie close in her arms. No man so proper for that sweet bed; no man may be so ready to die and mingle with her.

Maurice Hewlett.

Walt's Friend

(From *I sing the Body Electric*)

I KNEW a man, a common farmer, the
   father of five sons,
And in them the fathers of sons, and in them
   the fathers of sons.
This man was of wonderful vigour, calmness,
   beauty of person,

The shape of his head, the pale yellow and white of his hair and beard, the immeasurable meaning of his black eyes, the richness and breadth of his manners,

These I used to go and visit him to see, he was wise also,

He was six feet tall, he was over eighty years old, his sons were massive, clean, bearded, tan-faced, handsome,

They and his daughters loved him, all who saw him loved him,

They did not love him by allowance, they loved him with personal love,

He drank water only, the blood show'd like scarlet through the clear-brown of his face.

He was a frequent gunner and fisher, he sail'd his boat himself, he had a fine one presented to him by a ship-joiner, he had fowling-pieces presented to him by men that loved him,

When he went with his five sons and many grandsons to hunt or fish, you would pick him out as the most beautiful and vigorous of the gang,

You would wish long and long to be with him, you would wish to sit by him in the boat that you and he might touch each other. *Walt Whitman.*

Tom Sueter

(From *The Cricketer's Guide*)

WHAT a handful of steel-hearted soldiers are in an important pass, such was Tom in keeping the wicket. Nothing went by him; and for coolness and nerve in this trying and responsible post, I never saw his equal. As a proof of his quickness and skill, I have numberless times seen him stump a man out with Brett's tremendous bowling. Add to this valuable accomplishment, he was one of the manliest and most graceful of hitters. Few would cut a ball harder at the point of the bat, and he was, moreover, an excellent short runner. He had an eye like an eagle—rapid and comprehensive. He was the first who departed from the custom of the old players before him, who deemed it a heresy to leave the crease for the ball; he would get in at it, and hit it straight off and straight on; and, egad! it went as if it had been fired. As by the rules of our club, at the trial-matches no man was allowed to get more than thirty runs, he generally gained his number earlier than any of them. I have seldom seen a handsomer man than Tom Sueter, who measured about five feet ten. As if, too, Dame Nature wished to show at his birth a specimen of her prodigality, she gave him so amiable a disposition, that he was the pet of all the neighbourhood: so honourable a heart, that his word was never questioned by the gentlemen who associated with him; and a voice, which for sweetness, power, and purity of tone (a tenor) would, with proper cultivation, have made him a handsome fortune. With what rapture have I hung upon his notes when he has given us a hunting song in the club-room after the day's practice was over. . . . Lear was a short man, of a fair complexion, well looking, and of a pleasant aspect. He had a sweet counter tenor voice. Many a treat have I had in hearing him and Sueter join in a glee at the "Bat and Ball" on Broad Halfpenny:

> I have been there, and still would go;
> 'Twas like a little Heaven below!

John Nyken.

Uncle an' Aunt

HOW happy uncle us'd to be
   O' zummer time, when aunt an' he
O' Zunday evemens, yarm in yarm,
Did walk about ther tiny farm,
While birds did zing, an' gnats did zwarm,
Droo grass a'most above ther knees,
An' roun' by hedges an' by trees
   Wi' leafy boughs a-swayen.

His hat wer broad, his cuoat wer brown,
Wi' two long flaps a-hangèn down,
An' from his knee went down a blue
Knit stockèn to his buckled shoe,
An' aunt did pull her gown-tail droo
Her pocket-hole, to keep en neat,
As she mid walk, or teäke a seat
 By leafy boughs a-swayen.

An' vust they'd goo to zee their lots
O' pot-yarbs in the geärden plots;
An' he, i'-maybe, gwain droo hatch
Would zee aunt's vowls upon a patch
O' zeeds, an' vow if he could catch
Em wi' his gun, they shoudden vlee
Noo mwore into their roostèn tree,
 Wi' leafy boughs a-swayen.

An' then vrom geärden tha did pass
Drough archet var to zee the grass.
An' if the blooth, so thick an' white,
Mid be at al a-touch'd wi' blight,
An' uncle, happy at the zight,
Did guess what cider there mid be
In al the archet, tree wi' tree,
 Wi' tutties all a-swayen.

An' then tha stump'd along vrom there
A-vield, to zee the cows an' meare;
An' she, when uncle come in zight,
Look'd up, an' prick'd her yers upright,

An' whicker'd out wi' al her might;
An' he, a-chucklen, went to zee
The cows below the shiädy tree,
   Wi' leafy boughs a-swayen.

An' last ov al, they went to know
How vast the grass in meäd did grow
An' then aunt zed 'twer time to goo
In huome, a holdèn up her shoe
To show how wet 'e wer wi' dew.
An' zoo they toddled huome to rest,
Lik' culvers vlee-en to ther nest
   In leafy boughs a-swayen.

William Barnes.

Will Wimble

AS I was yesterday morning walking with Sir Roger before his house, a country fellow brought him a huge fish, which, he told him, Mr. William Wimble had caught that very morning; and that he presented it with his service to him, and intended to come and dine with him. At the same time he delivered a letter, which my friend read to me as soon as the messenger left him.

"SIR ROGER—I desire you to accept of a jack, which is the best I have caught this season. I intend to come and stay with you a week, and see how the perch bite in the Black

River. I observe with some concern the last time I saw you upon the bowling-green that your whip wanted a lash to it; I will bring half a dozen with me that I twisted last week, which I hope will serve you all the time you are in the country. I have not been out of the saddle for six days last past, having been at Eton with Sir John's eldest son. He takes to his learning hugely.—I am, Sir, Your humble servant, WILL WIMBLE."

This extraordinary letter and message that accompanied it made me very curious to know the character and quality of the gentleman who sent them, which I found to be as follows:— Will Wimble is younger brother to a baronet, and descended of the ancient family of the Wimbles. He is now between forty and fifty; but being bred to no business and born to no estate, he generally lives with his elder brother as superintendent of his game. He hunts a pack of dogs better than any man in the country, and is very famous for finding out a hare. He is extremely well versed in all the little handicrafts of an idle man. He makes a May-fly to a miracle, and furnishes the whole country with angle-rods. As he is a good-natured, officious fellow, and very much esteemed upon account of his family, he is a wel-

come guest at every house, and keeps up a
good correspondence among all the gentlemen
about him. He carries a tulip root in his
pocket from one to another, or exchanges a
puppy between a couple of friends that live
perhaps in the opposite sides of the county.
Will is a particular favourite of all the young
heirs, whom he frequently obliges with a net
that he has weaved, or a setting-dog that he
has made himself. He now and then presents
a pair of garters of his own knitting to their
mothers or sisters, and raises a great deal of
mirth among them by inquiring as often as
he meets them "how they wear"! These
gentleman-like manufactures and obliging little
humours make Will the darling of the country.
Addison's "Spectator."

A Gentleman of the Old School

HE lived in that past Georgian day,
   When men were less inclined to say
That "Time is Gold," and overlay
      With toil their pleasure;
He held some land, and dwelt thereon,—
Where, I forget,—the house is gone;
His Christian name, I think, was John,—
      His surname, Leisure.

Reynolds has painted him,—a face
Filled with a fine, old-fashioned grace,
Fresh-coloured, frank, with ne'er a trace
    Of trouble shaded;
The eyes are blue, the hair is drest
In plainest way,—one hand is prest
Deep in a flapped canary vest,
    With buds brocaded.

He wears a brown old Brunswick coat,
With silver buttons,—round his throat,
A soft cravat;—in all you note
    An elder fashion,—
A strangeness, which to us who shine
In shapely hats,—whose coats combine
All harmonies of hue and line,
    Inspires compassion.

He lived so long ago, you see!
Men were untravelled then, but we,
Like Ariel, post o'er land and sea
    With careless parting;
He found it quite enough for him
To smoke his pipe in "garden trim,"
And watch, about the fish tank's brim,
    The swallows darting.

He liked the well-wheel's creaking tongue,—
He liked the thrush that stopped and sung,—
He liked the drone of flies among
    His netted peaches;

He liked to watch the sunlight fall
Athwart his ivied orchard wall;
Or pause to catch the cuckoo's call
    Beyond the beeches.

His were the times of Paint and Patch,
And yet no Ranelagh could match
The sober doves that round his thatch
    Spread tails and sidled;
He liked their ruffling, puffed content,—
For him their drowsy wheelings meant
More than a Mall of Beaux that bent,
    Or Belles that bridled.

Not that, in truth, when life began
He shunned the flutter of the fan;
He too had maybe "pinked his man"
    In Beauty's quarrel;
But now his "fervent youth" had flown
Where lost things go; and he was grown
As staid and slow-paced as his own
    Old hunter, Sorrel.

Yet still he loved the chase, and held
That no composer's score excelled
The merry horn, when Sweetlip swelled
    Its jovial riot;
But most his measured words of praise
Caressed the angler's easy ways,—
His idly meditative days,—
    His rustic diet.

Not that his "meditating" rose
Beyond a sunny summer doze;
He never troubled his repose
    With fruitless prying;
But held, as law for high and low,
What God withholds no man can know,
And smiled away enquiry so,
    Without replying.

We read—alas, how much we read!—
The jumbled strifes of creed and creed
With endless controversies feed
    Our groaning tables;
His books—and they sufficed him—were
Cotton's *Montaigne*, *The Grave* of Blair,
A "Walton"—much the worse for wear,
    And *Aesop's Fables*.

One more—*The Bible*. Not that he
Had searched its page as deep as we;
No sophistries could make him see
    Its slender credit;
It may be that he could not count
The sires and sons to Jesse's fount,—
He liked the "Sermon on the Mount,"—
    And more, he read it.

Once he had loved, but failed to wed,
A red-cheeked lass who long was dead;
His ways were far too slow, he said,
    To quite forget her;

And still when time had turned him gray,
The earliest hawthorn buds in May
Would find his lingering feet astray,
    Where first he met her.

In Coelo Quies heads the stone
On Leisure's grave,—now little known,
A tangle of wild-rose has grown
    So thick across it;
The "Benefactions" still declare
He left the clerk an elbow-chair,
And "12 Pence Yearly to Prepare
    A Christmas Posset."

Lie softly, Leisure! Doubtless you,
With too serene a conscience drew
Your easy breath, and slumbered through
    The gravest issue;
But we, to whom our age allows
Scarce space to wipe our weary brows,
Look down upon your narrow house,
    Old friend, and miss you!
              Austin Dobson.

Mr. Hastings
(From *Forest Scenery*)

MR. HASTINGS was low of stature, but very strong, and very active; of a ruddy complexion, with flaxen hair. His cloaths were always of green cloth. His house was of the old fashion; in the midst of a large park, well stocked with deer, rabbits, and fish-ponds. He had a long narrow bowling-green, in it; and used to play with round sand-bowls. Here too he had a banqueting-room built, like a stand, in a large tree. He kept all sorts of hounds, that ran buck, fox, hare, otter, and badger; and had hawks of all kinds, both long, and short winged. His great hall was commonly strewed with marrow-bones; and full of hawk-perches, hounds, spaniels, and terriers. The upper end of it was hung with fox-skins of this, and the last year's killing. Here and there a pole-cat was intermixed; and hunter's poles in great abundance. The parlour was a large room, compleatly furnished in the same stile. On a broad hearth, paved with brick, lay some of the choicest terriers, hounds, and spaniels. One or two of the great chairs, had litters of cats in them, which were not to be disturbed. Of these three or four always attended him at dinner; and a little white wand lay by his trencher, to defend it, if they were too troublesome. In the windows, which were very large, lay his arrows, cross-bows, and other accoutrements. The corners of the room were filled with his best hunting and hawking poles. His oister-table stood at the lower end of the room, which was in constant use twice a day, all the year round; for he never failed to eat oisters both at dinner, and supper; with which the neighbouring town of Pool supplied him. At the upper end of the room stood a small table with a double desk; one side of which held a church-bible; the other, the book of martyrs. On different tables in the room lay hawk's hoods; bells; old hats, with their crowns thrust in, full of pheasant eggs; tables; dice; cards; and store of tobacco-pipes. At one end of this room was a door, which opened into a closet; where stood bottles of strong beer, and wine; which never came out but in single glasses, which was the rule of the house; for he never exceeded himself; nor permitted others to exceed. Answering to this closet, was a door into an old chapel; which had been long disused for devotion; but in the pulpit as the safest place, was always to be found a cold chine of beef, a venison-pasty, a gammon of bacon, or a great apple-pye, with thick crust, well-baked. His table cost him not much, tho' it was good to eat at. His sports supplied all, but beef and mutton; except on Fridays when he had the best of fish. He never wanted a London pudding; and he always sang it in with, *My part lies therein-a*. He drank a glass or two of wine at meals; put syrup of gilly-flowers into his sack; and had always a tun-glass of small-beer standing by him, which he often stirred about with rosemary. He lived to be an hundred; and never lost his eyesight, nor used spectacles. He got on horseback without help; and rode to the death of the stag, till he was past fourscore.

William Gilpin.

Jack

1

EVERY village has its Jack, but no village ever had quite so fine a Jack as ours:—
So picturesque,
Versatile,
Irresponsible,
Powerful,
Hedonistic,
And lovable a Jack as ours.

2

How Jack lived none knew, for he rarely did any work.
True, he set night-lines for eels, and invariably caught one,
Often two,
Sometimes three;
While very occasionally he had a day's harvesting or hay-making.

And yet he always found enough money for tobacco,
With a little over for beer, though he was no soaker.

3

Jack had a wife.
A soulless, savage woman she was, who disapproved volubly of his idle ways.
But the only result was to make him stay out longer,
(Like Rip Van Winkle).

4

Jack had a big black beard, and a red shirt, which was made for another,
And no waistcoat.
His boots were somebody else's;
He wore the Doctor's coat,
And the Vicar's trousers.
Personally, I gave him a hat, but it was too small.

5

Everybody liked Jack.
The Vicar liked him, although he never went to church.
Indeed, he was a cheerful Pagan, with no temptation to break more than the Eighth Commandment, and no ambition as a sinner.

The Curate liked him, although he had no
   simpering daughters.
The Doctor liked him, although he was never
   ill.
I liked him too—chiefly because of his perpetual good temper, and his intimacy with
   Nature, and his capacity for colouring
   cutties.
The girls liked him, because he brought them
   the first wild roses and the sweetest
   honeysuckle;
Also, because he could flatter so outrageously.

6

But the boys loved him.
They followed him in little bands:
Jack was their hero.
And no wonder, for he could hit a running
   rabbit with a stone,
And cut them long, straight fishing-poles and
   equilateral catty forks;
And he always knew of a fresh nest.
Besides, he could make a thousand things
   with his old pocket-knife.

7

How good he was at cricket too!
On the long evenings he would saunter to the
   green and watch the lads at play,

And by and by some one would offer him a few knocks.

Then the Doctor's coat would be carefully detached, and Jack would spit on his hands, and brandish the bat,

And away the ball would go, north and south and east and west,

And sometimes bang into the zenith.

For Jack has little science:

Upon each ball he made the same terrific and magnificent onslaught,

Whether half volley, or full pitch, or long hop, or leg break, or off break, or shooter, or yorker.

And when the stumps fell he would cheerfully set them up again, while his white teeth flashed in the recesses of his beard.

8

The only persons who were not conspicuously fond of Jack were his wife, and the schoolmaster, and the head-keeper.

The schoolmaster had an idea that if Jack were hanged there would be no more truants;

His wife would attend the funeral without an extraordinary show of grief;

And the head-keeper would mutter, "There's one poacher less."

9

Jack was quite as much a part of the village
  as the church spire;
And if any of us lazied along by the river in
  the dusk of the evening—
Waving aside nebulæ of gnats,
Turning head quickly at the splash of a jump-
  ing fish,
Peering where the water chuckled over a
  vanishing water-rat—
And saw not Jack's familiar form bending
  over his lines,
And smelt not his vile shag,
We should feel a loneliness, a vague impres-
  sion that something was wrong.

10

For ten years Jack was always the same,
Never growing older,
Or richer,
Or tidier,
Never knowing that we had a certain pride in
  possessing him.
Then there came a tempter with tales of
  easily acquired wealth, and Jack went
  away in his company.
He has never come back,

And now the village is like a man who has lost an eye.

In the gloaming, no slouching figure, with colossal idleness in every line, leans against my garden wall, with prophecies of the morrow's weather;

And those who reviled Jack most wonder now what it was they found fault with.

We feel our bereavement deeply.

The Vicar, I believe, would like to offer public prayer for the return of the wanderer.

And the Doctor, I know, is a little unhinged, and curing people out of pure absence of mind.

For my part, I have hope; and the trousers I discarded last week will not be given away just yet.   *E. V. Lucas.*

The Vicar

SOME years ago, ere time and taste
   Had turn'd our parish topsy-turvy,
When Darnel Park was Darnel Waste,
   And roads as little known as scurvy,
The man who lost his way, between
   St. Mary's Hill and Sandy Thicket,
Was always shown across the green,
   And guided to the Parson's wicket.

Back flew the bolt of lissom lath;
　Fair Margaret, in her tiny kirtle,
Led the lorn traveller up the path,
　Through clean-clipt rows of box and myrtle
And Don and Sancho, Tramp and Tray,
　Upon the parlour steps collected,
Wagged all their tails, and seem'd to say,—
　"Our master knows you—you're expected."

Uprose the Reverend Dr. Brown,
　Uprose the Doctor's winsome marrow;
The lady laid her knitting down,
　Her husband clasp'd his ponderous "Barrow";
Whate'er the stranger's caste or creed,
　Pundit or Papist, saint or sinner,
He found a stable for his steed,
　And welcome for himself, and dinner.

If, when he reach'd his journey's end,
　And warm'd himself in Court or College,
He had not gain'd an honest friend
　And twenty curious scraps of knowledge,—
If he departed as he came,
　With no new light on love or liquor,—
Good sooth, the traveller was to blame,
　And not the Vicarage, nor the Vicar.

His talk was like a stream, which runs
　With rapid change from rocks to roses.

It slipt from politics to puns,
   It passed from Mahomet to Moses;
Beginning with the laws which keep
   The planets in their radiant courses,
And ending with some precept deep
   For dressing eels, or shoeing horses.

He was a shrewd and sound Divine,
   Of loud Dissent the mortal terror;
And when, by dint of page and line,
   He 'stablish'd Truth, or startled Error,
The Baptist found him far too deep;
   The Deist sigh'd with saving sorrow;
And the lean Levite went to sleep,
   And dream'd of tasting pork to-morrow.

His sermon never said or show'd
   That Earth is foul, that Heaven is gracious
Without refreshment on the road
   From Jerome, or from Athanasius:
And sure a righteous zeal inspired
   The hand and head that penn'd and plann'd them,
For all who understood admired,
   And some who did not understand them.

He wrote, too, in a quiet way,
   Small treatises, and smaller verses,
And sage remarks on chalk and clay,
   And hints to noble Lords—and nurses;

True histories of last year's ghost,
    Lines to a ringlet, or a turban,
And trifles for the *Morning Post,*
    And nothings for Sylvanus Urban.

He did not think all mischief fair,
    Although he had a knack of joking;
He did not make himself a bear,
    Although he had a taste for smoking;
And when religious sects ran mad,
    He held, in spite of all his learning,
That if a man's belief is bad,
    It will not be improved by burning.

And he was kind, and loved to sit
    In the low hut or garnish'd cottage,
And praise the farmer's homely wit,
    And share the widow's homelier pottage:
At his approach complaint grew mild;
    And when his hand unbarr'd the shutter,
The clammy lips of fever smiled
    The welcome which they could not utter.

He always had a tale for me
    Of Julius Cæsar, or of Venus;
From him I learnt the rule of three,
    Cat's cradle, leap-frog, and *Quae genus:*
I used to singe his powder'd wig,
    To steal the staff he put such trust in,
And make the puppy dance a jig,
    When he began to quote Augustine.

Alack the change! in vain I look
  For haunts in which my boyhood trifled,—
The level lawn, the trickling brook,
  The trees I climb'd, the beds I rifled:
The church is larger than before;
  You reach it by a carriage entry;
It holds three hundred people more,
  And pews are fitted up for gentry.

Sit in the Vicar's seat: you'll hear
  The doctrine of a gentle Johnian,
Whose hand is white, whose tone is clear,
  Whose phrase is very Ciceronian.
Where is the old man laid?—look down,
  And construe on the slab before you,
"*Hic jacet* GVLIELMOS BROWN,
  Vir nullâ non donandus lauru."
            Winthrop Mackworth Praed.

The Fiddler of Dooney

WHEN I play on my fiddle in Dooney,
    Folk dance like a wave of the sea;
My cousin is priest in Kilvarnet,
  My brother in Maharabuiee.

I passed my brother and cousin:
  They read in their books of prayer;
I read in my book of songs
  I bought at the Sligo fair.

When we come at the end of time,
  To Peter sitting in state,
He will smile on the three old spirits,
  But call me first through the gate;

For the good are always the merry,
  Save by an evil chance,
And the merry love the fiddle,
  And the merry love to dance:

And when the folk there spy me,
  They all come up to me,
With "Here is the fiddler of Dooney!"
  And dance like a wave of the sea.
                    W. B. Yeats

A HANDFUL OF PHILOSOPHY

SANCHO PANZA'S PROVERBS.

There is still sun on the wall.

It requires a long time to know any one.

All sorrows are bearable if there is bread.

He who does not rise with the sun does not enjoy the day.

Every one is as God made him, and very often worse.

Until death, all is life.

Praying to God and hammering away.

The world is too much with us; late and soon,
Getting and spending, we lay waste our powers;
Little we see in Nature that is ours;
We have given our hearts away, a sordid boon!
This Sea that bares her bosom to the moon;
The winds that will be howling at all hours,
And are up-gathered now like sleeping flowers;
For this, for every thing, we are out of tune;
It moves us not.—Great God! I'd rather be
A Pagan suckled in a creed outworn;
So might I, standing on this pleasant lea,
Have glimpses that would make me less forlorn;
Have sight of Proteus rising from the sea;
Or hear old Triton blow his wreathèd horn.

William Wordsworth.

Content

Art thou poor, yet hast thou golden slumbers?
   O sweet content!
Art thou rich, yet is thy mind perplexéd?
   O punishment!
Dost thou laugh to see how fools are vexéd
To add to golden numbers, golden numbers?
O sweet content! O sweet, O sweet content!

 Work apace, apace, apace, apace;
 Hence labour bears a lovely face;
Then hey nonny nonny, hey nonny nonny!

Canst drink the waters of the crispéd spring?
   O sweet content!
Swimm'st thou in wealth, yet sink'st in thine own tears?
   O punishment!
Then he that patiently want's burden bears
No burden bears, but is a king, a king!
O sweet content! O sweet, O sweet content!

 Work apace, apace, apace, apace;
 Honest labour bears a lovely face;
Then hey nonny nonny, hey nonny nonny!
     Thomas Dekker.

The Wish

WELL then; I now do plainly see,
　　This busy world and I shall ne'er
　　　　agree;
The very honey of all earthly joy
　　Does of all meats the soonest cloy,
　　And they, methinks, deserve my pity,
Who for it can endure the stings,
The crowd, and buzz, and murmurings
　　Of this great hive, the city.

Ah, yet, ere I descend to th' grave
May I a small house and large garden have!
And a few friends, and many books, both true,
　　Both wise, and both delightful too!
　　And since love ne'er will from me flee,
A mistress moderately fair,
And good as guardian-angels are,
　　Only belov'd, and loving me!

O fountains, when in you shall I
Myself, eased of unpeaceful thoughts, espy?
O fields! O woods! when, when shall I be made
　　The happy tenant of your shade?
　　Here's the spring-head of pleasure's flood;
Where all the riches lie, that she
　　Has coin'd and stamp'd for good.

Pride and ambition here,
Only in far-fetched metaphors appear;
Here nought but winds can hurtful murmurs
    scatter,
    And nought but echo flatter.
The gods, when they descended, hither
From heav'n did always choose their way;
And therefore we may boldly say,
    That 'tis the way too thither.

How happy here should I,
And one dear she live, and embracing die!
She who is all the world, and can exclude
    In deserts solitude.
I should have then this only fear,
Lest men, when they my pleasure see,
Should hither throng to live like me,
    And make a city here.
Abraham Cowley.

Give Me the Old 〜 〜 〜 〜

Old wine to drink, old wood to burn, old books to read, and old friends to converse with.

I

OLD wine to drink!—
    Ay, give the slippery juice,
That drippeth from the grape thrown loose,
    Within the tun;

Pluck'd from beneath the cliff
Of sunny-sided Teneriffe
  And ripened 'neath the blink
    Of India's sun!
  Peat whisky hot
Tempered with well-boiled water!
These make the long nights shorter—
    Forgetting not
Good stout old English porter.

II

  Old wood to burn!—
Ay, bring the hill-side beech
From where the owlets meet and screech,
    And ravens croak;
The crackling pine, and cedar sweet;
Bring too, a clump of fragrant peat,
  Dug 'neath the fern;
    The knotted oak,
  A faggot too, perhaps,
Whose bright flame, dancing, winking,
Shall light us at our drinking;
  While the oozing sap
Shall make sweet music to our thinking.

III

  Old books to read!—
Ay, bring those nodes of wit

The brazen-clasped, the vellum writ,
　Time-honoured tomes!
The same my sire scanned before
The same my grandshire thumbèd o'er
The same his sire homeward bore,
　The well-earned meed
　　Of Oxford's domes:
　　Old Homer blind,
Old Horace, rake Anacreon, by
Old Tully, Plautus, Terence lie;
Mort Arthur's olden minstrelsie
Quaint Burton, quainter Spenser, ay,
And Gervase Markham's venerie—
　　Nor leave behind
The Holy Book by which we live and die.

IV

　Old friends to talk!—
Ay, bring those chosen few,
The wise, the courtly, and the true,
　　So rarely found;
Him for my wine, him for my stud,
Him for my easel, distich, bud,
　　In mountain walk! [1]
　　　　　　Robert H. Messinger.

---

[1] Two lines omitted.

To-Morrow

IN the downhill of life, when I find I'm declining,
  May my fate no less fortunate be
Than a snug elbow-chair will afford for reclining,
  And a cot that o'erlooks the wild sea;
With an ambling pad-pony to pace o'er the lawn,
  While I carol away idle sorrow,
And blithe as the lark that each day hails the dawn
  Look forward with hope for To-morrow.

With a porch at my door, both for shelter and shade too,
  As the sunshine or rain may prevail;
And a small spot of ground for the use of the spade too,
  With a barn for the use of the flail:
A cow for my dairy, a dog for my game,
  And a purse when a friend wants to borrow;
I'll envy no Nabob his riches or fame,
  Or what honours may wait him To-morrow.

From the bleak northern blast may my cot be completely
  Secured by a neighbouring hill;

And at night may repose steal upon me more sweetly
  By the sound of a murmuring rill:
And while peace and plenty I find at my board,
  With a heart free from sickness and sorrow,
With my friends may I share what To-day may afford,
  And let them spread the table To-morrow.

And when I at last must throw off this frail cov'ring
  Which I've worn for three-score years and ten,
On the brink of the grave I'll not seek to keep hov'ring,
  Nor my thread wish to spin o'er again:
But my face in the glass I'll serenely survey,
  And with smiles count each wrinkle and furrow;
As this old worn-out stuff, which is threadbare To-day,
  May become everlasting To-morrow.
                            John Collins.

A Thanksgiving to God

LORD, thou hast given me a cell
    Wherein to dwell;
A little house, whose humble roof

        Is weather proof;
Under the spars of which I lie
        Both soft and dry;
Where thou, my chamber for to ward,
        Hast set a guard
Of harmless thoughts, to watch and keep
        Me, while I sleep.
Low is my porch, as is my fate;
        Both void of state;
And yet the threshold of my door
        Is worn by th' poor,
Who thither come, and freely get
        Good words, or meat.
Like as my parlour, so my hall
        And kitchen's small;
A little buttery, and therein
        A little bin,
Which keeps my little loaf of bread
        Unchipt, unflead;
Some brittle sticks of thorn or briar
        Make me a fire,
Close by whose living coal I sit,
        And glow like it.
Lord, I confess too, when I dine,
        The pulse is thine,
And all those other bits that be
        There placed by thee:
The worts, the purslain, and the mess
        Of water-cress,

Which of thy kindness thou hast sent;
    And my content
Makes those, and my belovèd beet,
    To be more sweet.
'Tis thou that crown'st my glittering hearth
    With guiltless mirth,
And giv'st me wassail bowls to drink,
    Spiced to the brink.
Lord, 'tis thy plenty-dropping hand
    That soils my land,
And giv'st me, for my bushel sown,
    Twice ten for one;
Thou mak'st my teeming hen to lay
    Her egg each day;
Besides, my healthful ewes to bear
    Me twins each year;
The while the conduits of my kine
    Run cream, for wine:
All these, and better, thou dost send
    Me, to this end,—
That I should render, for my part,
    A thankful heart;
Which, fired with incense, I resign,
    As wholly thine;
—But the acceptance, that must be,
    My Christ, by Thee.

Robert Herrick.

The Dirge in "Cymbeline"

FEAR no more the heat o' the sun
    Nor the furious winter's rages;
Thou thy worldly task hast done,
    Home art gone and ta'en thy wages:
Golden lads and girls all must,
As chimney-sweepers, come to dust.

Fear no more the frown o' the great:
    Thou art past the tyrant's stroke;
Care no more to clothe and eat;
    To thee the reed is as the oak:
The sceptre, learning, physic, must
All follow this, and come to dust.

Fear no more the lightning-flash,
    Nor the all-dreaded thunder-stone,
Fear not slander, censure rash;
    Thou hast finished joy and moan:
All lovers young, all lovers must
Consign to thee, and come to dust.

No exorciser harm thee!
Nor no witchcraft charm thee!
Ghost unlaid forbear thee!
Nothing ill come near thee!
    Quiet consummation have;
    And renowned be thy grave!
                  William Shakespeare.

THE RETURN

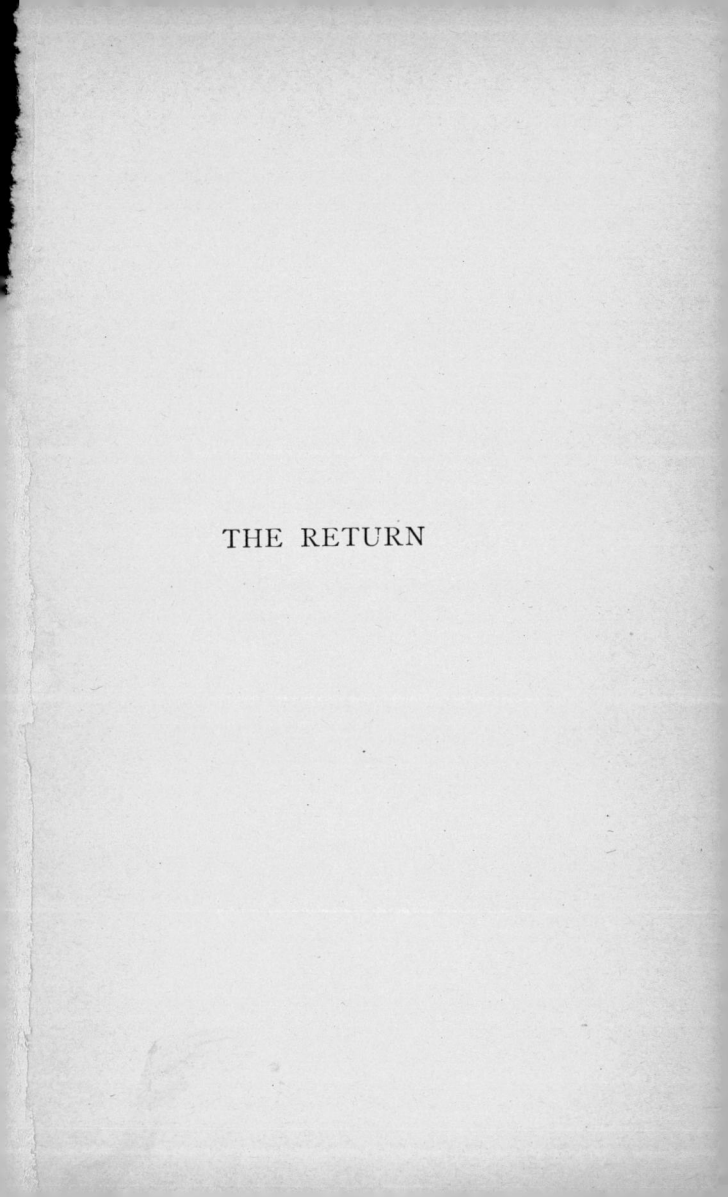

The Glamour of the Town

LET them talk of lakes and mountains and romantic dales—all that fantastic stuff; give me a ramble by night, in the winter nights in London—the Lamps lit—the pavements of the motley Strand crowded with to and fro passengers—the shops all brilliant, and stuffed with obliging customers and obliged tradesmen—give me the old bookstalls of London—a walk in the bright Piazzas of Covent Garden. I defy a man to be dull in such places — perfect Mahometan paradises upon earth! I have lent out my heart with usury to such scenes from my childhood up, and have cried with fullness of joy at the multitudinous scenes of Life in the crowded streets of ever dear London. . . . I don't know if you quite comprehend my low Urban Taste; but depend upon it that a man of any feeling will have given his heart and his love in childhood and in boyhood to any scenes where he has been bred, as well to dirty streets (and smoky walls as they are called) as to green lanes, "where live nibbling sheep," and to the everlasting hills and the Lakes and ocean. A mob of men is better than a flock of sheep, and a crowd of happy faces jostling into the playhouse at the hour of six is a more beautiful spectacle to man than the shepherd driving his "silly" sheep to fold.

Charles Lamb to Robert Lloyd.

NOTE

THANKS are due to many authors and publishers for their kindness in permitting in this book the use of copyright poems and prose passages: to Mrs. Hinkson for two lyrics from *The Wind in the Trees* (Grant Richards); to Miss Nora Hopper; to Mrs. Meynell for extracts from *The Rhythm of Life, The Colour of Life, The Spirit of Place,* and *Poems* (all published by Mr. Lane), and for " The Lady of the Lambs"; to Mr. Charles Baxter for quotations from R. L. Stevenson's *Songs of Travel, Travels with a Donkey,* and *The Merry Men* (Chatto and Windus); to the Rev. H. C. Beeching for poems from *In a Garden* (Lane); to Mr. Robert Bridges for two numbers from his *Shorter Poems* (Bell and Sons); to Mr. John Burroughs for a passage on the apple from *Winter Sunshine* (David Douglas in England, and Houghton, Mifflin, and Co., in America); to Mr. Bliss Carman for poems from *Songs from Vagabondia* and *More Songs from Vagabondia,* two of which are from his own pen, and two from that of his collaborator, Mr. Richard Hovey (Elkin Mathews, in England, and Small, Maynard and Co., in America); to Mr. John Davidson for a passage from his *Fleet Street Eclogues* (Lane); to Mr. Bertram Dobell for two songs from the selection of James Thomson's poems recently made and published by him; to Mr. Austin Dobson for poems from *Old World Idylls* and *At the Sign of the Lyre* (both published by Messrs. Kegan Paul and Co.); to Mr. Kenneth Grahame for extracts from *Pagan Papers* (Lane); to Messrs. Houghton, Mifflin, and Co., for two of Whittier's poems; to Mr. A. E. Housman for two extracts from *A Shropshire Lad* (Grant Richards); to Mr. Maurice Hewlett for good sentiments from *Pan and the Young Shepherd* (Lane); to Mr. Le Gallienne for lyrics from *Robert Louis Stevenson* and *English Poems* (both published by Mr. Lane); to Messrs. Longmans for a passage from Richard Jefferies' *Story of My Heart;* and to the same publishers and the Executors of Mr. William Morris for two extracts from *Poems by the Way;* to Messrs. Macmillan for lyrics from the late T. E. Brown's *Old John* and Miss Rossetti's *Poems;* to Mr. William Sharp for a quotation from Philip Bourke Marston's *Song Tide* (Scott); to Messrs. Small, Maynard and Co., and to Mr. Horace L. Traubel, one of Walt Whitman's literary executors, for extracts from *Leaves of Grass;* to the Misses Smith for a song by the late Ada Smith; to Mr. Swinburne for "A Match," from his *Poems and Ballads,* First Series (Chatto and Windus); to Mrs. Francis Thompson for "A May Burden" from his *New Poems* (Constable); to Mr. William Watson for two songs from his *Collected Poems* (Lane); and to Mr. W. B. Yeats for lyrics from his *Poems* (Fisher Unwin) and *The Wind among the Reeds* (Elkin Mathews).

UP-HILL

Does the road wind up-hill all the way?
   Yes, to the very end.
Will the day's journey take the whole long day?
   From morn to night, my friend.

But is there for the night a resting place?
   A roof for when the slow dark hours begin.
May not the darkness hide it from my face?
   You cannot miss that inn.

Shall I meet other wayfarers at night?
   Those who have gone before.
Then must I knock, or call when just in sight?
   They will not keep you standing at the door.

Shall I find comfort, travel-sore and weak?
   Of labour you shall find the sum.
Will there be beds for me and all who seek?
   Yes, beds for all who come.

Christina G. Rossetti